RISING UP

Same Subject, Different Narratives

RISING UP

The Power Of Narrative
In Pursuing Racial Justice

SONALI KOLHATKAR

Foreword By Rinku Sen

CITY LIGHTS BOOKS — OPEN MEDIA SERIES
SAN FRANCISCO

"Brilliant, compelling, and inspiring hope, *Rising Up* lays bare the ways that narratives shape our lives—sometimes by obscuring or normalizing oppressive systems, and other times by demanding a paradigm shift for imagining and building towards a more just world. Like her ground-breaking journalism, Sonali Kolhatkar's book spotlights voices across various news, entertainment, and social-media platforms that exemplify movement building for racial justice through troubling narratives. This book could not come at a better time—let's all read, discuss, and act on it today!"

—**KEVIN KUMASHIRO**, Ph.D., author of *Surrendered: Why Progressives are Losing the Biggest Battles in Education*

"Sonali Kolhatkar's *Rising Up: The Power of Narrative in Pursuing Racial Justice* could just as easily be called *Changing Assumptions*. This book looks at the narratives that have been created through the course of building the USA as a racial settler state, narratives that have led to the adoption of an assortment of assumptions, including by victims of racial settler-colonialism. The book challenges the reader not only to rethink these assumptions, but to understand the critical importance of the creation of progressive narratives as an instrument in the struggles for human liberation. I was drawn in immediately!"

—**BILL FLETCHER JR.**, author of *"They're Bankrupting Us": And Twenty Other Myths about Unions*

"Sonali Kolhatkar reminds us we are the stories we tell. Our stories can cast a spell of hate, division, and fear, or they can break the powerful grip of racial injustices that have held us since our country's beginning. With personal and collective wisdom, Kolhatkar guides us in the storytelling that liberates."

—**LUIS J. RODRIGUEZ**, author of *Always Running*

"For two decades, Sonali Kolhatkar has been a leading voice for truth against the lies of the powerful, unflinchingly exploding prevailing myths that pass as prevailing wisdom. She understands that shifting the narrative is radical anti-racist work, and if you don't believe it just look at the firing of schoolteachers and journalists for telling the truth about racism, slavery, gender, or Palestine. The answer is not the *New York Times* or MSNBC but independent media and an educated, engaged populace. *Rising Up* offers a clear path forward."

— **ROBIN D. G. KELLEY**, author of *Freedom Dreams: The Black Radical Imagination*

"In this incisive analysis on storytelling and power, Kolhatkar takes us on a deep dive into how US media either reinforces or dismantles the racist narratives that are at the foundation of this nation. A brilliantly outlined argument for independent media's historic role in humanizing those who have been othered through the society's architectures of power, *Rising Up* highlights the crucial work of courageous storytelling in combating white supremacy and building a more just world."

— **RUPA MARYA**, co-author of *Inflamed: Deep Medicine and the Anatomy of Injustice*

"Foundational and guiding, Sonali's book gifts us a piercing map of the dangers of illegitimate stories, as well as a guide towards the unrelenting power of truthful ones. This is the book I have been waiting for. Read it. Share it. And we shall surely rise."

— **DR. ORIEL MARÍA SIU**, author of *Christopher the Ogre Cologre, It's Over!*

"Conceptualizing the terrain of storytelling as a dynamic, complex one that is constantly open to new forms of radical, autonomous, collective mobilization, *Rising Up* is a reinvigorated call for journalism, art, and aesthetics that advance abolitionist, decolonizing, and anti-racist movements."

— **DYLAN RODRÍGUEZ**, author of *White Reconstruction: Domestic Warfare and the Logic of Racial Genocide*

Open Media Series Editor: Greg Ruggiero
Cover and text design: Patrick Barber
Cover photo: © Copyright Drazen Zigic/Shutterstock.com

ISBN-13: 9780872868724

Library of Congress Cataloging-in-Publication Data
Names: Kolhatkar, Sonali, author. | Sen, Rinku, author of foreword.
Title: Rising up : the power of narrative in pursuing racial justice / Sonali
    Kolhatkar : foreword by Rinku Sen.
Description: San Francisco : City Lights Books, 2023. | Series: Open media
Identifiers: LCCN 2022052686 | ISBN 9780872868724 (trade paperback)
Subjects: LCSH: Racism in popular culture—United States. | Racism in
    mass media—United States. | Social justice in popular culture—United
    States. | Social justice—United States. | United States—Race relations.
    | Narration (Rhetoric).
Classification: LCC E184.A1 K725 2023 | DDC 305.80073—dc23/
    eng/20230112
LC record available at https://lccn.loc.gov/2022052686

City Lights Books are published at the City Lights Bookstore
261 Columbus Avenue, San Francisco, CA 94133

citylights.com

CONTENTS

Stop thinking about saving your face. Think of our lives and tell us your particularized world.

Make up a story. Narrative is radical, creating us at the very moment it is being created.

We will not blame you if your reach exceeds your grasp; if love so ignites your words they go down in flames and nothing is left but their scald. Or if, with the reticence of a surgeon's hands, your words suture only the places where blood might flow. We know you can never do it properly—once and for all. Passion is never enough; neither is skill. But try.

     —**TONI MORRISON**, Nobel Lecture
      December 7, 1993

FOREWORD   By Rinku Sen

HE'D BEEN STROLLING BACK AND FORTH BETWEEN THE shelves, around the edges of a few rows of folding chairs. I was at Powell's in Portland, Oregon, a gem of a bookstore, with my co-author Fekkak Mamdouh, to give a reading from *The Accidental American*, our 2008 book about Mamdouh's life as an immigrant organizer. Afterwards, the thin young man with short brown hair whom I had noticed earlier, came and spoke to me. He looked like a perfectly ordinary American.

"I was listening to your talk," he said. "You write about immigration? I have a question. I graduated high school a couple of years ago and found out that I couldn't go to college. I couldn't get a job. I was up here looking at the architecture books because that's what I want to do."

"I'm illegal," he whispered to me. "I'm wondering, is there something I could do? Should I go to the authorities and turn myself in?"

If this had been a right-wing sting operation by the likes of James O'Keefe, there would be video of me telling this man not to turn himself in to immigration authorities, that a deportation was very likely, but that there was hope that the Obama administration might change the rules. I suggested he get involved with organizations comprised of other young undocumented immigrants, and told him that in lots of places they were fighting for things like the DREAM Act, which would let undocumented students go to colleges by paying in-state tuition, and for new immigration laws that would allow people to adjust their residency status.

More than anything, I was struck by how the young man labeled himself "illegal," a dehumanizing term that relegated him to the status of "other." Every couple of years since my early activist days, the idea of getting rid of the word "illegal" to describe immigrants came up in my social circles. In 2008, after promising immigration reform bills had failed to pass and subsequent bills were watered down but still failed to pass, as deportations began ramping up even under a Democratic administration, as a young man whispered "I'm illegal" before naming his broken dreams, it felt like the time had come. So, Colorlines.com and the Applied Research Center (later renamed Race Forward) launched the "Drop the I-word" campaign to push the Associated Press to revise its style guide.

Not everyone was enthusiastic. Some of the major immigrant rights groups declined to join us; they were focused on improving legislation and were skeptical about the campaign's viability. At least one independent outlet decided not to sign on because it was, "too much advocacy, too little objectivity." When resources are tight—as they undoubtedly were at the start of the housing market crash—people tend to gravitate toward concrete matters. Changing the words that newspapers use didn't seem that important, especially since success seemed unlikely.

And yet we won. Once AP dropped the word, so did the *LA Times* and *USA Today*. This effort to refocus the immigration debate on actual human beings was only one of many such actions and campaigns. In 2010, four undocumented young people walked from Florida to Washington, DC, as part of what was called the Trail of Dreams. A year later, acclaimed journalist José Antonio Vargas came out as undocumented in the *New York Times Magazine*. That same year, immigrant teens with United 4 the Dream protested the I-word in front of the offices of the *Charlotte Observer*. And in 2012, the National Hispanic Media Coalition found that, even when presented with positive images of Latinos, audiences still equated "Latino" with "illegal" at rates of 47 percent and higher, depending on the platform.

Narrative change involves adding to or replacing the themes and ideas that are embedded in collections of stories. When I was growing up, these themes and ideas were often called the "moral of the story," a characterization that still works for me. When many people repeat these stories in multiple forms for decades or more, the morals become part of a society's "common sense" norms that everyone knows by shorthand and symbol.

If this kind of change sounds like painstaking work, especially on racial justice, there are many examples in my lifetime that we can point to where accepted narratives were shaken. These include ideas like "marriage is between a man and a woman," "wife-beating is a private matter," and "smoking is good for you."

The hard work, methodical yet inspired, of community leaders, scientists, organizers, witnesses, writers, artists, producers, researchers, teachers, reporters, and funders replaced these bits of supposed common sense with "love is love," "domestic violence is a public crime," and "smoking kills," respectively.

I used to look at such transformations and wonder what magic had enabled them. What manner of artistic innovation? Which heroic witnesses? What serendipitous confluence of events had converted the public view on fundamental questions of human survival and governance?

Now, I know that it isn't magic. Or if magic, it is the kind cooked up by millions of people creating every day. Creating care. Creating solutions. Creating stories.

Much remains to be done, especially on abolishing narratives that perpetuate racial hierarchy. In this important and timely book, Sonali Kolhatkar offers an inspired vision for how we can identify, challenge, and ultimately change oppressive narratives.

The great thing about narrative organizing, Sonali reminds us, is that all of us can do it. Telling stories is our birthright as human beings. We're already constantly narrating the world around us, placing ourselves or others in tales with morals. We can go along with "common sense" or what others claim is the dominant narrative. But if "common sense" is neither widely held nor effective for a community, we've got choices. This book highlights how to choose wisely.

Stories are most often passed through conversation. The most popular movie in the world would have little effect if people didn't talk about it, or act on its implications and then brag about that. This narrative ability is a more accessible form of power than the economic or political kind. Thus, it often drives the transitions from fighting and losing to fighting and winning.

When we ignore this power, when we fail to nurture it, we allow ourselves to be named and positioned in ways that continue to oppress us.

Grounded in years of hands-on reporting, Sonali's analysis offers inspiration and instruction to rise up for racial justice now. The people we meet in *Rising Up* recognize this relationship between narrative power and political strategy. They believe, as I do, as Sonali does, that racial justice is indeed achievable, and they will use any available tool to make it so.

The nation did not get immigration reform from the "Drop the I-word" campaign, nor from two terms of the Obama administration. But it did get DACA, the Deferred Action for Childhood Arrivals program. I would like to imagine that the would-be architect I met in Portland in 2008 used the DACA process to get a social security number and a work permit. That he went to school and eventually dropped the "would-be" from his professional identity. That he fell in love, started a family, and today contributes daily to his community, as do 800,000 people just like him.

Prometheus transferred fire away from gods to mortals, but we don't need a Prometheus. We transfer narrative power from the few to the many by claiming it and using it, in revolutionary acts that both catalyze the national consciousness and transform material conditions.

We win what we narrate, and we win more when we narrate together.

PREFACE

AS A JOURNALIST, MY VALUES—CLICHÉ AS THIS MAY SOUND—
are "to afflict the comfortable and comfort the afflicted." By definition,
journalists are truthtellers called upon to honestly report the facts in the
service of the public interest and justice. What ethic could serve the
public more than the pursuit of justice for all human beings regardless
of race, gender, or class?

I've been engaged in narrative work via journalism for more than
twenty years. In 2002, I abandoned a job working on a satellite telescope at the prestigious California Institute of Technology (Caltech),
and set my sights on a path of independent journalism grounded in the
pursuit of justice—a path that felt much more meaningful to me than a
career in astrophysics.

Much as I enjoyed the beauty and challenges of addressing grand cos-
mological questions, journalism is in my blood. My grandfather, the late
Shripad Yashwant Kolhatkar—an Indian rebel, freedom fighter, trade
unionist, and co-founder of the Communist Party of India (Marxist)—
also served as president of the All-India Newspaper Employees Federa-
tion. I feel the strength of his legacy even though he passed away before I
found my true calling.

Here's how it happened. As an immigrant preteen growing up in
Dubai, I wrote for a local children's magazine called *Young Times*. I

interviewed fellow students, wrote stories, and created drawings, but had not yet considered journalism as a potential career. I went on to study physics and astronomy, emigrating to the United States on a foreign student visa at the age of sixteen, convinced that I would end up with a long career in science. After graduating, I started working at Caltech, fixated on the grand questions of physical existence on the astronomical scale. But around the same time, I grew increasingly cognizant of the injustices in the world around me and of how little progress we had made to solve the grand problems of humanity right here on Earth. I became deeply involved in solidarity work with Afghan feminists and gave public lectures about the US war in Afghanistan.

When an opportunity arose to be a regular news broadcaster at the independent community station KPFK, the Pacifica Radio outlet in Los Angeles, I jumped at the chance. Since then, I have spent over two decades reporting the indignities faced by marginalized communities and covering the contours of their resistances through my television and radio program, *Rising Up With Sonali*.

Today, as the racial justice editor at *Yes! Magazine*, I also have the privilege of uplifting Black and Brown voices via print and online media. The mission of my labor is to help tell their stories, amplifying the efforts of people of color who are working to create a world based on justice, freedom, equity, love, and community.

The late congressman and civil rights icon John Lewis once said, "The movement without storytelling, is like birds without wings." As a cultural worker grounded in social justice advocacy, I have always seen my journalism as a vehicle for transformative storytelling about people and power. The mere fact that I, an immigrant woman of color, am in the position of being a public storyteller, is radical in a world where women of color are constantly excluded from positions of editorial leadership. My liberation is bound up with the liberation of the people whose stories I share. By becoming fluent in each other's stories, we rise up against racism. Through solidarity, we rise up together.

RISING UP

INTRODUCTION   Driving Like an Asian

SOME YEARS AGO, I WENT GROCERY SHOPPING WITH MY son in a middle-class neighborhood of Pasadena, California, where I live. My four-year-old sat in the front section of the shopping cart, his little legs dangling, as we chatted, shopped, and ticked things off my list. When I stopped to pick up a bag of apples, I noticed that a tall white man was impatiently trying to move past me while muttering something that included the word "Asian."

I asked, "Excuse me? What was that?"

The man, who was apparently in a hurry and had decided that my pace was slowing him down, proceeded to yell, "You're driving like an Asian! Why don't you go back to your country?"

At first I was confused. *Driving?* I wondered. *In a grocery store?* Then I realized he was engaging in a racist attack. With indignation clouding my mind and stunting my ability to eloquently retort, I raised my voice and demanded that the staff throw him out.

When the store manager confronted the man, he accurately recounted his words to her—including his insult that I was "driving like an Asian."

"Well, at least he's an honest racist," I thought to myself.

After he left, the store manager apologized to me and asked me to forget the whole thing ever happened. A white woman who had witnessed the altercation came up to me and said she was glad I stood up to him, and that if she had been in my place, she would have punched him.

I continued walking around the store in a daze, picking up produce with trembling hands, attempting to finish shopping as calmly as I could while assuring my bewildered child that all was well.

That incident took place in July 2013, just days after I had covered a story on my radio show of how a Florida man named George Zimmerman was acquitted in a trial for the murder of Trayvon Martin, an African American teenager.

Zimmerman had described the seventeen-year-old Martin to police as a "real suspicious guy," and suggested that he might be "on drugs or something." An encounter that started with Zimmerman thinking "something was off" about a Black teenager in a hoodie walking on the street, ended with him snuffing out the teen's life.

Being constantly targeted by racist aggression is an all-too-common experience for people of color in the United States. The dynamic generates a persistent anxiety that anytime we are in public, judgments based on our race can make us vulnerable to humiliation, trauma, and violence. Many of us live in a semi-constant state of fear.

After I finished shopping and left the store, my phone rang with an unrecognized local number. For a split second, fear bubbled up reflexively. I imagined it was the racist from the store tracking me down, taking his harassment to the next level. It turned out to be someone from my doctor's office confirming an appointment.

And then I was angry.

I was livid at the man for exercising power over me. I seethed at my fellow shoppers for not standing up for me as they witnessed the whole incident unfold, staying silent when they might have sympathized with me. I was outraged that the store manager tolerated the incident and asked me to simply forget about it instead of trying to hold the perpetrator accountable in some way. And finally, I was angry for not standing up for myself more strongly.

When this white man encountered me, his racist assumptions about my ethnic background—including the stereotype that all Asians are bad drivers—formed the basis of a narrative that rationalized his verbal violence.

Similarly, we can surmise that Zimmerman harbored false assumptions based on his perceptions of Martin and the false stereotype that most Black male teenagers are potential criminals. Those assumptions—and the racist narratives they reinforce—drove his act of deadly violence.

In between the extremes of our two encounters—I walked away somewhat traumatized but alive, but Martin never got to see his eighteenth birthday—exist countless routine acts of violence framed by narratives that perpetuate racial hierarchy and power in America today.

But the country is changing. America of color is growing quickly, white America is not. By 2045, white Americans will be a racial minority.[1] Meanwhile, communities of color face growing levels of reactionary repression, violence, and legislative attacks on our education, freedom, and electoral power. And, of course, we remain under-represented in the halls of power.

As this book illustrates, Black and Brown people across the United States are fighting back. We are rising up to tell our stories in *our* way. We are rising up to challenge racist stereotypes and shift narratives about who we are, using every means at our disposal, whether through mass media or social media, academia or cultural education. Not only is shifting the narrative an increasingly critical part of racial justice organizing, it is central to changing the nation's collective consciousness in the long term. "More and more institutions working to eliminate oppressive systems and build inclusive ones are coming to understand that stories and storytelling are the backbone of an inclusive society," as Shanelle Matthews, founder of Radical Communicators Network, said. "How they're told defines whose lives are valued and whose are not," she added, "and *that* narrative power shapes all other types of power, such as social power, economic power, and political power."[2]

Understanding Race and Racist Stereotypes

It has often been said that race is a social construct. Whole books have been written to explore this idea, but it's not very complicated. Race can be thought of as a perceived difference between humans of different ethnic backgrounds and ancestral lineages. Such perceptions are often based on whiteness as a metric of normalcy, and extend as far as the depth of melanin in our skin cells, sometimes to the shape of our nose, the slant of our eyes, the kinks and colors of our hair strands, the manner of our speech, the spelling of our names.

In other words, race is a superficial aspect of who we are as humans. And yet it is the most visible aspect of who we are, and has long been a basis for enforcing unjust hierarchies of power and privilege.

Those who have been trained to say "I don't see race" rely on the biological superficiality of race to claim that skin color doesn't inform their thought processes and fuel stereotypes. They are often lying to themselves and to everyone else. While they clearly see visible racial markers, they choose to ignore the gross injustice of existing racial hierarchies.

Those hierarchies are built on the edifices of stereotypes—simplistic reductions of people based on distorted generalizations. From a racist's viewpoint, I am an Asian, and therefore I am a bad driver and among the "immigrant hordes" invading the country to steal a job from a more deserving native-born citizen. I am a stingy tipper, a "Tiger Mom," and my food smells and tastes too strong. I'm unhygienic and carry disease (a popular stereotype during the COVID-19 pandemic) or I'm a religious fanatic who hates America (a common trope after the 9/11 attacks). The perpetuation of such falsehoods provides a basis for racialized aggression, vigilantism, and the normalization of harassment of people of color like me.

Narrative = Story + Intention

"Narrative imagining—story—is the fundamental instrument of thought," explained Mark Turner, a cognitive scientist and linguist, in his book *The Literary Mind*. "Rational capacities depend upon it. It is our chief means of looking into the future, of predicting, of planning, and of explaining."[3]

Although the word "narrative" is often distilled as simply a "story," within a social and political context, a narrative can be seen as a story that is imbued with the values of the storyteller and told with intention. If one's intention is to achieve racial justice and equity, here's how ReFrame explains it can be done, in a piece by Jen Soriano, Joseph Phelan, Kimberly Freeman Brown, Hermelinda Cortés, and Jung Hee Choi: "When narrative strategy is integrated into organizing, impacted communities can expand the public notion of what is possible. Larger narratives, in dynamic relationship with individual stories, help people see personal experiences as part of a larger arc, inspiring collective action and building consensus and power toward social change."[4]

A narrative may be deliberately false or partly true, and the narrator's intention may be an attempt to disinform and manipulate others or to educate and empower them, and everything in between. For example, narratives that promote the criminality of Black or Hispanic people are used as justifications for racial disparities in police arrests, criminal convictions, and prison sentences. In contrast, narratives centered on racial justice and the humanity of people of color can form the basis of reforming our criminal justice system to be racially equitable. Reframe, Jen Soriano's narrative power organization, wants to "create a common sense where the structural forms of society can't be anything but liberatory"—a perfect summation of the future that racial justice narratives can help to build.[5]

Racist narratives are generally based on stereotypes, while racial justice narratives are based on our complex humanity. This is a central point, one that I will return to again and again throughout this book.

We can identify racist narratives by asking the following questions about the story and the storyteller's intention: Is the story based on stereotypes? Does it seek to preserve imbalances of power or to abolish them? Does the narrator hail from the community that they are telling stories about, or from outside?

If we look closely, we start to see false narratives based on racist stereotypes everywhere, including in supposedly liberal spaces—in the media, in political language, in books, movies, television shows, social media, and popular culture.

Confronting Racist Narratives

White supremacy propagates false and destructive narratives about people of color being defective, criminal, lazy, invasive, violent, parasitic, one-dimensional; white people are cast as normal, deserving, noble, complex, vulnerable, and independent.

The story of my encounter in the grocery store offers an example that fits squarely within prevalent white supremacist narratives that people of color are inferior, don't deserve to be treated the same as white Americans, and should return to the countries of their ancestors.

According to a race-based analysis from the National Center for Statistics and Analysis in 2009, Asians, Native Hawaiians, and Pacific Islanders are the safest drivers among all ethnic groups, with the lowest rates of accidents.[6]

In spite of this, to the racist man in the grocery store, I was "driving like an Asian" because he likely saw himself as a superior driver by virtue of his whiteness, and me as an inferior one by virtue of being Asian. His verbal attack was a stark reminder that people like him enjoy racial privilege over people like me.

There are countless such false narratives perpetuated throughout our culture that feed—and are fueled by—racism. In fact, my grocery store encounter was on the very mild end of the spectrum of racist attacks. But, if left unaddressed, such narratives will continue to impede the trajectories of our lives, stymieing our ability to live with dignity and thrive, as so many Asians victimized by racist violence during the coronavirus pandemic have found out. In the most dangerous contexts—as when people of color encounter police, armed vigilantes, white supremacist terrorists—racist narratives can lead to murder.

Today, racist narratives remain strong in right-wing politics, culture, and media. They also remain simmering beneath the surfaces of most liberal institutions and will continue to do so until and unless they are challenged. Such narratives need to be confronted, dismantled, and replaced with ones built on the foundations of our diverse and joyful humanity. If we don't make this happen, our children will grow up to face the same cruelty and violence that we have been forced to endure.

Racial Equity: The Goal of Narrative Work

The goal of narrative-shifting is to change public consciousness to the degree necessary for society to achieve justice. Part of that involves changing policy, but policy alone is not enough. What does a racially just society look like? The answer is not complicated or mystifying. In fact, part of it can be found under most of our noses, buried in so-called DEI initiatives that are increasingly popular in workplaces.

In the months following the police killing of George Floyd, corporate workplaces and government agencies tackled the upheaval with internal discussions on racial justice through the lens of "Diversity, Equity, and Inclusion" or DEI. Diversity and inclusion are easy enough to achieve but do little to challenge white supremacy. However, the 'E' in DEI initiatives is where meaningful change happens.

So, for example, powerful institutions have, for years, loved the idea of "diversity" as a way to illustrate their generosity. Think of the "United Colors of Benetton" ads of the 1980s that featured models of different skin tones wearing Benetton-branded clothing. Diversity is a nicer word for "tokenism," a branding effort to sidestep addressing deeper matters of institutional racism.

"Inclusion" can also be toothless. All that an institution needs to do in order to fulfill the idea of inclusion is to include a person of color. For example, the US Supreme Court can claim to be an inclusive institution by the mere presence of the ultra-conservative African American justice Clarence Thomas. But Thomas's position did not increase emancipatory conditions in the United States. Inclusivity, like diversity, can be tokenism by another name.

But then there's "equity," a quietly powerful word inserted in between two often co-opted ideas. Appearing on the surface as a distant cousin to the older idea of equality, equity has a much deeper meaning than equality, diversity, or inclusion. The term originates from the French word *équité*, which means justice or rightness.

Whereas equality means sameness or giving everyone the same opportunities, equity implies accounting for historical injustices.

Here is a specific example of how the two differ: Equality for Black people means removing official barriers to home ownership, education, health care, and more. But equity for Black people means reparations to compensate for centuries of enslavement, oppression, Jim Crow segregation, and ongoing systemic racism so that home ownership, quality education, and health care are actually within reach. Equality ignores the past. Equity addresses historical injustice. Glenn Harris, president of Race Forward and publisher of the news site Colorlines, explains that "racial equity is about applying justice and a little bit of common sense to a system that's been out of balance." Says Harris, "We achieve racial equity when race no longer determines one's socioeconomic outcomes; when everyone has what they need to thrive, no matter where they live."[7]

Racial equity requires a higher standard of justice than simple racial equality, diversity, or inclusion, because it requires a redistribution of power. In order to achieve true justice, nothing less will do.

Racial Justice Narratives

Returning to the topic of stereotyping Asian people, there are exceedingly few American television programs by and about Asian Americans. *Fresh Off the Boat* on ABC is one such rarity. In one episode Eddie, the show's teenage protagonist, begs his father, Louis, to teach him to drive.[8] At one point, Louis pulls over his car to help a white couple who seem to be having car trouble.

A white police officer stops to investigate and assumes that Louis has caused an accident by virtue of being Asian. He makes this assumption blithely while claiming he is not a racist. Louis walks away angry and confused and concludes that he would indeed teach his teenage son Eddie to drive, saying to him, "You're going to be the best damn driver on the road." It's a sentiment familiar to people of color. Our parents taught us that in order to avoid discrimination by white folk, we had work twice as hard and be twice as good.

This example forms a part of a growing movement by people of color to rewrite racist narratives in mass media and elsewhere. Despite the internet, television remains a powerful influence on our culture. While this white-dominated medium has generally spread racist stereotypes and damaging narratives about people of color, in this instance, an Asian-made television show chose to depict people with racist views about Asians, and then, more importantly, developed a counternarrative grounded in Louis's humanity.

When justice informs the stories told on television, such a medium can become an effective cultural tool in our arsenal to demolish the influence of white supremacy and help reclaim who we are as full human beings. This sort of narrative work can be done in many forms, including news media, film, television, social media, and even face-to-face conversations.

Narratives in Traditional Media

White supremacist forces in the United States understand the importance of controlling narratives. They have spread falsehoods for centuries about communities of color, using all available platforms. Their attacks come relentlessly and often proliferate faster than we can keep track of them. In Chapter 1 of this book, I explore the insidious ways that media outlets have promoted white supremacy. From Bob Grant and Rush Limbaugh to Sean Hannity and today's cast of characters on Fox News, right-wing media outlets are the launching pads for culture wars that deeply influence the nation and undermine social justice.

Meanwhile, the counterforce to the semi-fascist right-wing media outlets is the educated, if staid, professional liberal media universe: the *New York Times*, *Washington Post*, *Boston Globe*, *Guardian*, and so on. These commercial media operations, beholden to profit margins, are supposed to symbolize the bulwarks of reason and humanist values. They offer the best journalism that the corporate economy can muster. But, time and again, they perpetuate racist assumptions of white normalcy and fall far short of the crucial issues relevant to ordinary Americans.

Given that we cannot rely on the liberal corporate media to effectively counter right-wing corporate media, it falls to the perpetually underfunded independent nonprofit media to do the critically important narrative work of driving progress. Indeed, as shown in Chapter 2, independent media have been on the front lines of promoting racial justice time and again, daring to challenge power, expose injustice, and center the voices of communities of color in the process.

Narratives in Television and Film

Whether we admit it or not, our perceptions of social hierarchy are to a huge extent influenced by pop culture. On matters of race, this is especially true for white Americans living in segregated neighborhoods and for those whose encounters with Black and Brown people are mostly via the media.

As I lay out in Chapter 3, one of the media's biggest blind spots is police criminality and racism. Media institutions in the United States are deeply invested in police as noble purveyors of law and order. And Hollywood has helped this PR campaign for decades, nurturing the perception that police officers stand on the dividing line between order and anarchy—the lovable, yet tough, baton wielders of justifiable force and state power. Such "copaganda" has served as an external reinforcement of the "Blue Wall of Silence" and has preserved the dehumanization of police victims—disproportionately Americans of color.

But, as Chapter 4 shows, young and talented filmmakers of color such as Ryan Coogler and Ava DuVernay are changing the calculus of storytelling in Hollywood, inserting deeply nuanced, three-dimensional portraits of Black and Brown people into the film pantheon. Activist organizations and academics have called out Hollywood in systematic ways, including studies such as the Hollywood Diversity Report and campaigns like #OscarsSoWhite. When creators of color control the reins of storytelling, the results are stunning, with growing diversity of roles and story lines that are only just beginning to even the scales and shift narratives.

Narratives in Individual Discourse

Today, social media have become an effective platform for citizen journalists to creatively address urgent social issues. In Chapter 5, I explore how the phenomenon known as "Black Twitter" is articulating the collective sensibilities of a community that has been disproportionately excluded from traditional media. The subject of numerous studies, Black Twitter has emerged as an unignorable tool for drawing national attention to racial violence and injustices against people of color, shaping narratives around police aggression, calling out institutional injustice, and organizing mass protests and mobilizations. Newer platforms are constantly emerging, and apps such as TikTok are increasingly important in creating a space for the cultural and political expressions of young people of color.

But organized or not, social media are often a messy means for narrative-shifting, and frequently remain under elite corporate control. In Chapter 6, I examine traditional person-to-person narrative work done on a micro level by educators of color to upend white supremacist myths and train young people to apply a critical racial justice lens to society. I also profile activists such as Loretta Ross, whose work promotes "calling-in" culture—a way to engage in effective narrative-shifting through love and engaged discourse.[9] We'll also see how advocacy organizations such as People's Action are applying this idea on a broader scale, using an old-school, in-person technique dubbed "deep canvassing" to help change people's minds toward progressive values on race and related issues.

Rising Up to Reclaim Our Stories

While writing this book, I often found myself thinking of bell hooks and the lens she developed to view the world. As a young journalist in my twenties, I avidly read the work of the famed cultural critic and insurgent theorist who so eloquently and fiercely questioned illegitimate power, always grounding her vision in justice and love. In her 1992 collection of essays, *Black Looks: Race and Representation*, hooks wrote, "There is a direct and abiding connection between the maintenance of white supremacist patriarchy in this society and the institutionalization via mass media of specific images, representations of race, of blackness, that support and maintain the oppression, exploitation, and overall domination of all Black people."[10] Today the idea that narrative work and culture-shifting are necessary parts of our movements has started to enter our collective consciousness, and hooks was an early pioneer of such efforts.

My purpose in writing this book is to help readers develop a radar for racist narratives in the mass media, particularly in corporate news, Hollywood films, and television shows. By delving into the insidious narratives that these white-dominated industries perpetuate, the book reveals the built-in assumptions that we are meant to internalize, and exposes the intentional harm they cause. I hope by the end readers will find that they can better identify racist narratives and demand counter-narratives that dignify people of color.

My intention is also to focus on the systematic efforts by people of color, working from the outside, to pressure these industries and, infiltrating them against all odds, to push for change from within. Their efforts are a growing measure of the demographic change in American society.

And finally, I want to convince you, the reader, that the work of promoting truthful stories grounded in our humanity is a critical, often ignored tool for achieving racial justice that we all can participate in as individuals.

Our experiences directly inform the kinds of stories we tell. As an immigrant woman of color, I have faced many attacks over the years based on racist perceptions—the "go back to your country" variety being the most common. My gender, complexion, accent, and foreign-sounding name have all garnered varying responses of resentment from those seeking to marginalize me. Verbal abuse, electronic abuse, casual racism and sexism, and even threats are constant and personal reminders of the work that remains to be done.

In recalling that incident at the grocery store years ago, I remember thinking that my brown-skinned children might one day be subjected to the same harassment. For the sake of all our sons and daughters who remain relegated to the status of "others" in white-dominated America, we must be relentless in rewriting public narratives. As scholar and writer john a. powell, director of the Othering and Belonging Institute at the University of California, Berkeley, said, "How we do race will be consequential to the kind of society we have in the future.... Our future will be impacted by the way the conscious and unconscious make meaning of our new social constructions [of race]."[11]

Being a target of racism can be a useful qualification for doing narrative work on racial justice. But I see clearly that on an ongoing basis and historically, African Americans and Indigenous peoples are subjected to the most pervasive forms of injustice in the United States.

I will never know the lived experience of being Black in America, a nation that generated immense wealth on enslavement and that continues to systematically foist injustices upon its Black citizens. Similarly, I will never fully understand the lived experience of Indigenous people in this country, what historical trauma, family separation, and genocide have wrought on generations, and how the legacy of colonialism persists today in dangerous and toxic ways.

As a non-Black, non-Indigenous woman of color, it is critically important for me—and others like me—to collectively uplift Black and Indigenous voices and center them in the narrative work we must all do to further racial justice. In the pages ahead, you will meet Black and Indigenous activists, academics, and storytellers, setting the standards for the transformation we seek. Until all are free, none of is are free.

As people of color grow in numbers, the racism of old narratives is being exposed, and new narratives are being written. Who gets to participate in the writing ultimately controls how power is distributed. There's no stopping this trajectory, and the narratives advancing racial justice are slowly but surely taking hold. We are rising up.

ONE FAUX NEWS VS. NEWS THAT'S FIT TO PRINT

THE FREE PRESS IS MEANT TO BE A CRITICAL BULWARK OF any democracy, informing citizens how to instruct politicians to represent them, investigating injustices to spur public action, and spotlighting stories of social, economic, and political interest. But media outlets have also historically perpetuated white-supremacist narratives and the racist system they reinforce.

Today, right-wing media outlets have made it a key aspect of their agenda to propagate hateful myths about people of color, while accusing the rest of the media of having bias. In response, mainstream media outlets such as the *Washington Post*, *New York Times*, and National Public Radio, who have their own histories of white-supremacist coverage and routinely went out of their way to appear "objective" and "balanced," failed to adequately counter the racist disinformation and authoritarianism of right-wing media.

As I will illustrate later in this chapter, Donald Trump, who symbolizes the worst features of the modern Republican Party, directly benefited from such a media landscape, with one set of platforms blowing wind into his sails and the rest refusing to call out his racism until it was too late.

Grant's Rants

Robert Gigante routinely referred to Black people as "savages." Gigante was not the leader of an extremist hate group or a historical figure from hundreds of years ago. Instead, using the bland-sounding moniker Bob Grant, he spent decades in prime-time radio slots, including a stint from 1984 to 1996 on WABC, a radio station in New York owned by Capital Cities/Walt Disney.

Grant was a pioneer of combative right-wing talk radio. In 1986, he interviewed Bernhard Goetz, a white man who became famous for shooting four young Black men two years earlier on a New York City subway after they allegedly demanded five dollars from him. Three of his victims recovered, but the fourth, eighteen-year-old Darrell Cabey, was paralyzed and permanently brain damaged after Goetz shot him point-blank with his unlicensed pistol while the teenager cowered in a corner.[12]

Grant congratulated Goetz on the air, saying that he should have "finished the job by killing them all." The interview was typical of Grant's radio program, which spewed racist epithets and degraded people of color for two and a half decades. Day after day, on his show Grant indoctrinated listeners with racist narratives about Black and Brown people, relentlessly portraying them as subhuman, criminal, and deserving of harm. He was largely lauded for his work.

In 1996, Grant was finally taken off the air for comments he made about the nation's first African American commerce secretary, Ron Brown, who died in a plane crash. Grant jokingly worried about the possibility that Brown might have been the only survivor—no one survived—and was fired over it.[13]

When asked why Grant had been allowed to remain on air for so many years, an unnamed ABC producer told the *New York Times*, "Our advertisers are aware that hate sells their products," and said that ultimately it boiled down to profits: "If the person has good ratings, a station has to overlook the garbage that he spews out."[14]

But we can hardly imagine a person of color being allowed to remain on air for decades while routinely denigrating white Americans—high ratings or not. Such are the standards of a racist system in a capitalist economy.

"Playful Bigotry"

Filmmaker Jen Senko knows the impact of Grant's hate in a real and visceral way. Her father, whom Senko describes as once being "very, very open-minded" and a "loving-everybody type of person," began listening to Grant on the radio during his daily commute.[15] That's when he began to change.

Senko made a documentary about her father called *The Brainwashing of My Dad*. In it, she charts how years of exposure to the narratives of Grant and others morphed him from a liberal to an angry, racist, conservative.

After he began listening to Grant's rants, Senko says, she began seeing her father say and do things that were "completely antithetical to what he used to be."[16]

Although Grant is not much of a household name anymore, his successor, Rush Limbaugh, still has name recognition. Limbaugh, a bombastic bigot, was the next influence on Senko's father, who began listening regularly to his racist and sexist radio programs. Senko saw that her once-peaceful father had, by then, turned into a very angry person. He had internalized the racist narratives that Grant and Limbaugh fed him and was filled with resentment toward people of color.

Limbaugh, who started his radio career on the same mainstream radio station as Grant—WABC in New York—remained deeply influential from the 1990s until his death in 2021. When asked to eulogize him, conservative commentator Charlie Sykes told NPR, "One of his contributions was playful bigotry."[17]

How fun.

Fairness and Accuracy in Reporting (FAIR), one of the few media watchdog groups that followed Limbaugh's work closely, documented his hate-filled rhetoric for years. Jeff Cohen, one of the group's cofounders, remembers how "stunned" he and his colleagues at FAIR were "when we were chronicling all of the crazy things this guy fed his audience day after day."[18]

Cohen describes Limbaugh's audience as "largely white male, middle-class [and] working-class" people who were devoted to him—people like Senko's father.[19]

But white women also found resonance with Limbaugh's politics. Kayleigh McEnany, a White House press secretary during Donald Trump's presidency, paid tribute to Limbaugh on Twitter when he died. Calling herself "the definition of a 'Rush Baby,'" McEnany fawned, "It's not just me. There are tens of thousands of us all across the conservative movement."[20] She added, "Rush inspired me at a young age, planting in my heart a passion for politics."[21]

That passion was shaped by the racist narratives that Limbaugh propagated for decades. For example, in 2012 she posted a tweet about President Barack Obama that invoked the racist conspiracy theory that he was not a US citizen by virtue of being Black with a foreign-sounding name: "How I Met Your Brother—Never mind, forgot he's still in that hut in Kenya. #ObamaTVShows."[22]

Conservative white Americans like McEnany and other Limbaugh fans went on to form the core audience of the most important, and perhaps most enduring, of all right-wing media outlets, Fox News.

It could be said that Grant begat Limbaugh, who begat Fox News.

Faux News

"It started back in 1964," says Senko, tracing the rise of right-wing media to its origins. "It was a sort of boomerang effect after [Barry] Goldwater lost to [Lyndon B.] Johnson in a landslide." Conservatives, worried about their waning influence, realized that one of the most effective ways to regain political power was to build their own media infrastructure in order to weave the kind of narratives that would drive voters to the polls.

"They had to paint the [existing] media as liberal and biased," and "develop their own media," says Senko.

And they did just that. Today, Fox News, whose relationship with the word "news" is tenuous at best, might be better labeled Faux News.

So successful did Fox News become that it spawned its own cottage industry of critics, including a 2004 documentary by Robert Greenwald, *Outfoxed: Rupert Murdoch's War on Journalism*, as well as a watchdog group called Media Matters for America, largely devoted to dissecting nearly every horrible thing that Fox News hosts have been saying for decades, up to the present day.

"Fox News is so racist you can categorize its racism," wrote researcher Dayanita Ramesh for the website Free Press.[23] Ramesh created a non-comprehensive list of the many people and groups that Fox targeted: Black Americans, Latinos, immigrants of color, women of color, Indigenous people, Asians, and Muslims, each group coming under unique forms of racist attacks.

If the views of nearly half of all conservatives in the US are shaped by an outlet that routinely weaves disparaging narratives about people of color, it is no wonder that by 2016 the time was ripe for a bombastic politician who manipulated voters using those same narratives to narrowly win the highest office in the nation.

Senko, like many other observers, sees a direct line between the rise of right-wing media and the rise of racist authoritarianism in the Republican Party. "This media created Donald Trump," she says. Indeed, Trump made no secret of how closely he consulted with Fox News hosts before making decisions.[24]

Conservatives have played the long game in creating their own media networks for social manipulation, indoctrination, and control. Doing so has resulted in the Republican Party being shaped by the white supremacy and disinformation of Donald Trump and those who fund him.

"Replacement Theory"

Fox News is not just the successor to hate radio's shock jocks—it is the multi-headed television spawn of the late, racist overlords of radio like Grant and Limbaugh. Sean Hannity, Laura Ingraham, and Jeanine Pirro are their modern-day technicolor reincarnations. Many others have come and gone, such as the uber-racist Bill O'Reilly, who was a popular Fox News host for more than twenty years before being fired. But none has been as overt in propagating white supremacist ideas as Tucker Carlson.

On May 14, 2022, an eighteen-year-old white man massacred ten people and injured three at a grocery store in Buffalo, New York. All those killed were Black. The perpetrator had published a manifesto online saying the victims were there to "ethnically replace my own people." The comments were a direct reference to Carlson's racist replacement narratives in which he claims that Democrats and the communities of color that vote for them are conspiring to replace white people, as a pathway to political power.[25]

A similar sentiment was heard five years earlier, when white nationalists marched in Charlottesville, Virginia, for their "Unite the Right" rally, bearing torches and chanting slogans such as "You will not replace us."[26] Although their chant was directed at the Jewish community, it has since broadened to include those who are not white or Christian.

The narrative that Carlson and others are propagating is that white Americans are facing an existential crisis at the hands of people of color, that *they* are the victims of an insidious project of erasure and domination, by Black and Brown people.[27] As a result, their reasoning goes, people of color must be stopped by any means necessary, including by building walls along the nation's borders, or, as the shooter in Buffalo did, by mass murder.

Genocidal Aspirations

If you say something often enough, it starts to sound true even if it's not.[28]

This sentiment is often attributed to Nazi propagandist Joseph Goebbels, who understood the power of disinformation and used it to deadly effect. Psychologists have studied the phenomenon, finding that if you say something patently untrue often enough, people will simply begin to believe it.

Today, right-wing media outlets—particularly Fox News—routinely make horrifying and dehumanizing claims about people of color. They repackage and repeat the disinformation in an endless loop, conditioning millions of their viewers to internalize racist narratives, with some becoming violent in the process.

Frank Meeink, a former neo-Nazi recruiter who was indoctrinated during his teenage years and convicted for violent crimes, eventually renounced his white supremacist views in prison after befriending Black inmates. In an interview with CNN about his 2021 book *Autobiography of a Recovering Skinhead*, Meeink said, "As a former radical, I can tell you from watching Fox News, I could show you where there's the same radical stuff that I used to say."[29]

He then remarkably compared Fox to media outlets in Rwanda whose role in whipping up the hatred that fueled the 1994 genocide is well documented. Meeink said, "If you look at Fox News and then you compare that to hate radio from Rwanda, and what started that civil war, there's comparisons there." Rwandan radio stations routinely degraded members of the Tutsi ethnic group, creating narratives that incited the horrors of the genocide.

When Fox News hired "Rush baby" McEnany as a regular contributor upon her departure from the White House, some of the outlet's own staff members were aghast. One unnamed staffer described McEnany to the Daily Beast as a "mini-Goebbels" who spewed "incessant lies from the White House."[30]

In a 2015 analysis for FAIR, researchers Sean McElwee and Jason McDaniel asked, "Does Fox News attract racist viewers, or is there something about Fox News that makes their viewers more racist?" They concluded, "The long history of race-baiting at Fox News raises suspicions that its coverage is indeed affecting its viewers' racial attitudes. More research needs to be done, but it appears that Fox News' connection to racial polarization may be a powerful one."[31] Even though there may not be an airtight case establishing that Fox News' disinformation directly increases hate crimes and acts of violence, the fact that it routinely engages in the sort of "playful bigotry" that Limbaugh was known for means that Fox's owners are profiting off racism.

"Liberal Media"

One of right-wing media's most enduring narratives is that "liberal media" exert too much influence over the nation. Conservatives, going back to Alabama governor George Wallace and later President Richard Nixon, have repeatedly rejected much mainstream media, claiming that they have an anti-conservative or liberal slant. Today, the very notions of racial justice and equality are cast as woke, socialist, or liberal rather than as fundamental tenets of a democratic society. Such an approach serves to blame the media rather than white supremacy.

In addition to blatantly far-right media like Fox News, there is an entire constellation of outlets that claim to be "objective" and to harbor neither liberal nor conservative bias. These media, however, also bear responsibility for tolerating and promoting white-supremacist views, often by bending over backwards to appease right-leaning attitudes, and sometimes even appealing directly to conservatives by hiring racist hosts.

For example, for years CNN gave Lou Dobbs a platform to spew his anti-immigrant hate. Dobbs was so virulently racist that the network was eventually shamed into firing him in response to a well-organized boycott organized by the Latino/a advocacy group Presente.org.[32]

Racism in Modern Media Coverage

In a 2017 study commissioned by the nonprofit organization Color of Change, Dr. Travis Dixon, a communications professor at the University of Illinois at Urbana-Champaign, analyzed the way major news media outlets covered the basic unit of US society—the family—from the start of 2015 to the end of 2016.[33] Dixon found that over the two-year period, media outlets routinely propagated racist narratives about families of color.

Black families in particular were portrayed as more likely to be poor and reliant on government welfare, by percentage and in comparison with white families, than they were in reality. Black parents were more likely to be reported as uninvolved or negligent compared to white parents. The media also over-represented Black people in general as criminals, compared to whites, who were under-represented as criminals.

Dixon concluded that such racist narratives drive racist treatment, saying, "There are dire consequences for Black people when these outlandish archetypes rule the day: abusive treatment by police, less attention from doctors, harsher sentences from judges, just to name a few."

If such coverage defines the "liberal media," we ought to be terrified of what "conservative media" represents. Rather than a spectrum that goes from far left to far right, today's mainstream media landscape occupies a range that goes from racist to even more racist.

When a Racist Is Not a Racist

The New York Times, long considered the paragon of "liberal media," boasts of featuring "all the news that's fit to print." While the *Times* routinely faces right-wing accusations of having a liberal bent, it has a history of enabling racist coverage—by assiduously avoiding calling out white supremacy and racism.

When, for example, Bob Grant was fired in 1996 for his racist remarks against the late commerce secretary Ron Brown, the *Times* painstakingly related Grant's many horrific racist comments in a detailed report, including his fantasy of drowning Haitian immigrants so they would stop coming to the United States. But the writers did not refer to him or his statements as racist. They only quoted Alan

Dershowitz using the r-word against Grant, and FAIR's then-senior analyst Steve Rendall referring to Grant's "hateful rhetoric."

When Grant died nearly eighteen years later, the *New York Times* still couldn't bring itself to call a spade a spade. In its obituary of Grant, the paper admitted that he was "boycotted for racist remarks," but the only adjectives that the writers used when referring to Grant personally were words like "combative" and "openly partisan."[34] To the paper he was simply a person who, over time, became "less constrained in talking about race."[35]

FAIR analyst Peter Hart later wrote that he found it "puzzling why the paper finds so many ways to describe Grant's racism instead of simply calling it what it was."[36]

Meanwhile, the *Times* had no qualms about labeling FAIR, in the same obituary, in clear terms as a "liberal-leaning watchdog group."[37]

Media that refuse to clearly identify the dehumanization of people of color are part of the problem, and the reluctance to call racists out is itself an act of racism. Silence is complicity, and the so-called "liberal media" have remained complicit in normalizing white supremacist perspectives for too long. The resulting narratives from such outlets have often been that racism is not such a big deal.

When Trump Wasn't Racist Enough

Donald Trump made it exceedingly clear right from the beginning of his presidential campaign what sort of leader he would be. On June 16, 2015, the day he launched his bid for the White House, Trump gave the speech in which he made his now-infamous comments: "When Mexico sends its people, they're not sending their best. They're not sending you. They're not sending you. They're sending people that have lots of problems, and they're bringing those problems with us. They're bringing drugs. They're bringing crime. They're rapists. And some, I assume, are good people."[38]

Such language is not ambiguous. Instead of labeling his 2015 speech as racist, which it clearly was, the *Washington Post* referred to his words as "inflammatory" and as "false comments connecting Mexican immigrants and crime."[39] The paper went to great lengths to fact-check whether or not most Mexican immigrants were actually drug dealers and rapists.

Such a shocking claim made by a presidential candidate shouldn't have required fact-checking. It should have been roundly denounced by all as blatant racism—and in fact, immigrant advocacy organizations and racial justice groups did just that.

Of course, Mexican immigrants are not more likely to be criminals than non-Mexicans—they are in fact less likely to be so. But the *Post* decided that it would take Trump's patently racist assertion seriously and prove it wrong with a detailed factual analysis—just in case the public was inclined to believe him.

While there is nothing wrong with fact-checking a racist statement—and it can help to point out the ludicrousness of racist beliefs—the fact that the *Washington Post* did so without labeling his words as clearly racist means that it did not consider the dehumanization of Mexicans sufficient cause to slap Trump with a label of "racist."

Perhaps if media outlets had clearly labeled Trump right from the start as a white supremacist, the Republican Party *might* have been too embarrassed to nominate him to lead the party, or at the very least, have been reluctant to do so.

The message that the failure to call out racists sends to those of us who are Black, Brown, Indigenous, Latina/o or Asian is that our humanity is of incidental importance, a negotiable factor in the pursuit of some vaguely defined idea of professional objectivity among white-dominated institutions.

Trump Finally Becomes a Racist—in 2019

It all came to a head when Trump, more than two years into his tenure, posted a denigrating and racist tweet about four newly elected progressive Congresswomen of color—Rashida Tlaib (D-MI), Ilhan Omar (D-MN), Alexandria Ocasio-Cortez (D-NY), and Ayanna Pressley

(D-MA).[40] "Why don't they go back and help fix the totally broken and crime infested places from which they came," Trump wrote.[41]

National Public Radio (NPR), another outlet that conservatives love to denigrate as the "liberal media," had generally refused to clearly identify racism and racist behavior in its reporting of Trump's campaign and presidency—until it became too embarrassing to remain silent. As the network grappled with the idea of calling a racist a racist, NPR's Keith Woods, who in 2019 was the vice president of Newsroom Diversity and Training, wrote an opinion piece advising that journalists should "report on racism" (what a relief!), but that they should "ditch the labels."[42] According to Woods, who is African American, journalists should not be in the business of "moral labeling."

Woods went further, saying that for journalists, "dispassionate distance is a virtue," and that such distance was "the fragile line that separates the profession from the rancid, institution-debasing cesspool that is today's politics."[43]

To Woods, it would debase the institution if journalism focused on calling out racism. It seemed as though Woods thought that if journalists began unequivocally identifying racism, everything would seem racist to them over time.

This stunningly flawed logic, coming from someone whose job title indicated that he was responsible for diversity in the newsroom (as of this writing, Woods's position is that of chief diversity officer for NPR), is a testament to just how flawed NPR remains when it comes to taking on racism even today.[44]

NPR eventually used the word "racist," and added the following note to Woods's op-ed as an indication of just how momentous an occasion it was: "NPR made the decision, this week, to call President Trump's tweets about a group of Democratic congresswomen, 'racist.'"

The Washington Post, another prominent member of the so-called "liberal media," also agonized over the decision to use the r-word in relation to Trump's tweet. Executive editor Martin Baron, apparently proud of the upstanding professionalism that his outlet showed in concluding that it was okay to say "racist," revealed that he had held a meeting with senior editors before doing so. Baron issued a public statement: "We had that discussion today about President Trump's use of a longstanding slur against African Americans and other minorities. The 'go back' trope is deeply rooted in the history of racism in the United States. Therefore, we have concluded that 'racist' is the proper term to apply to the language he used Sunday."[45]

Not only did it take major corporate media outlets more than two years of Trump's presidential tenure to begin labeling his person, actions, and words as racist, they boasted about just how much they grappled with the decision.

The message this sent is that it would take a great amount of overtly bigoted behavior for white people to earn the very serious label of "racist." But at least the narrative was changing.

"The money's rolling in and this is fun."

While some mainstream media outlets desperately wanted to apply professional detachment to Trump's hate, his incendiary racism translated into a financial windfall for their shareholders.

"Trump is fantastic for their ratings," says media analyst and author Victor Pickard, co-director of the Media, Inequality, and Change Center at the University of Pennsylvania. "He is money in the bank."[46]

David Bloom, media analyst for Forbes.com, concurred, writing in 2018 that "ratings and revenues have been great for many of Trump's biggest targets in the media."[47] Indeed, many outlets, including the *New York Times*, flourished in an era where near-daily provocations from the nation's leader provided fodder for outrage and analysis.

Recall that the Disney-owned radio station WABC had benefited from Bob Grant's overt racism in the 1980s and 1990s, prompting an ABC producer to say in 1996 that if a commentator gets good ratings, "a station has to overlook the garbage."[48]

There is little difference between this sentiment and one that CBS CEO Les Moonves expressed in February 2016 when Trump was making overtly racist statements. "Man, who would have expected the ride we're all having right now?" asked Moonves giddily. "It may not be good for America, but it's damn good for CBS," he said.[49]

He proceeded to encourage the presidential candidate to continue his shameful behavior, saying, "I've never seen anything like this, and this going to be a very good year for us. Sorry. It's a terrible thing to say. But, bring it on, Donald. Keep going."[50]

Moonves, a wealthy white man worth hundreds of millions of dollars, has paid little personal price for Trump's dehumanization of people of color.[51] To Moonves, "Donald's place in this election is a good thing."[52]

(For those us paying close attention to how he delighted in monetizing Trump's obscene remarks, it came as no surprise when, a few years later, Moonves was fired after half a dozen women accused him of sexual assault and harassment.[53])

But, just as WABC would very likely not have tolerated a host of color routinely degrading white people, it is impossible to imagine that CBS's Moonves would have delighted in the ratings bonanza of a Trump-like person of color running for president.

Racism is allowed to flourish not necessarily because it makes money for media owners, but because white America still dominates media and is invested in white-supremacist narratives. That racist content helps to generate profits is just an added bonus—a critical distinction.

"The money's rolling in and this is fun," Moonves said of Trump's obscene remarks.

And this is fun.

Protests or Riots? It Depends

Trump's racism was a crucial litmus test for mainstream corporate news outlets—one that largely revealed their tolerance for racism, especially in the first half of his presidential tenure. Although one could make a case, as did NPR's Woods, that "dispassionate distance is a virtue" among journalists, it turns out such distance is applied heavily when calling out racists, but not as much when reporting on racial justice protests. In coverage of Black Lives Matter protests, mainstream journalists seem to have little trouble in making moral judgments—against protesters.

This was confirmed by researcher Summer Harlow, who studies journalism at the University of Houston. Harlow and her colleagues examined how media outlets covered progressive social justice protests versus how they covered conservative protests, and concluded that "articles about conservative protests—like protests opposed to immigration or LGBT rights, or protests supporting Trump and gun rights—are less likely to be negatively framed as 'riots' than other types of protests."[54]

On the other hand, "Black Lives Matter protests are more likely to be framed as riots, as news coverage focuses more on violence, property damage, and confrontations with police," said Harlow in a summary of her findings.[55] This confirms existing racist narratives of Black people (and by extension, their allies) as out-of-control criminals and looters.

What's remarkable is that Harlow found a special disdain among journalists for racial justice protests compared to other progressive social movements. She noted, "Journalists were also less supportive of racial justice movements than they were of women's rights or immigrants' rights."[56]

Harlow found this bizarre behavior notable enough to conclude that "remaining objective was seemingly more important than taking an overt stance, even against racism."[57] How strange it is that to mainstream media outlets, racism—the treatment of human beings as less than human based on their skin color and national origin—is considered an opinion, not an affront to our modern-day understanding of human rights and equality.

It's hard not to conclude that such an approach is based on privilege and an investment in preserving white supremacy in media: the whiter the newsroom, the less interested journalists seem to be in taking a stand to assert the humanity of Black and Brown people.

"A National Reckoning with a Problem as Old as the Nation Itself"

When Officer Derek Chauvin slowly killed George Floyd in Minneapolis on May 25, 2020, in broad daylight, in full view of passersby, and on camera, white America was confronted with a glimpse of the reality that Black Americans have been facing for generations. Public outrage over the videotaped evidence catalyzed a national reckoning that continues to this day, prompting many news media to acknowledge the experiences of Americans of color more seriously, at least temporarily.

Moreover, when an estimated 15 to 26 million people in the United States took to the streets of more than 500 cities in the summer of 2020, enraged by the deaths of Floyd, Breonna Taylor, Daniel Prude, Ahmaud Arbery, and countless others, journalists had a front-row seat to police violence aimed at the protesters *and* at them.[58] The US Press Freedom Tracker found that "in a single year—from George Floyd's death during an arrest on May 25, 2020, to May 25, 2021—journalists were assaulted more than 600 times and arrested 155 times while reporting from Black Lives Matter protests across the country."[59] Meanwhile, in June 2020 the ACLU of Minnesota filed a lawsuit against multiple Minnesota law enforcement officials on behalf of a freelance journalist. According to documentation accompanying the lawsuit, "The protests were marked by an extraordinary escalation of unlawful force deliberately targeting reporters."[60]

As Elizabeth Hinton explained in her 2021 book *America on Fire: The Untold History of Police Violence and Black Rebellion Since the 1960s*, racist police brutality is not a new phenomenon and has triggered mass protest for generations. However, the spark for the latest chapter of protest can be traced to the 2014 uprising in Ferguson, Missouri, after the police killing of Black teenager Mike Brown. At that time, the mainstream media covered the Ferguson protests with little sensitivity to racial justice. For example, the *New York Times* published a lengthy postmortem of Brown's life saying he "was no angel, with public records and interviews with friends and family revealing both problems and promise in his young life."[61]

Racial justice advocates roundly denounced the paper for seemingly justifying his murder at the hands of a police officer. The tacit narrative that the *Times* crafted was that Brown was dispensable because he wasn't a productive, upstanding citizen, or that he somehow provoked the officer's attack and deserved it because of his past record.

Fast-forward to Floyd's videotaped killing in Minneapolis six years later. Although the number of Black people killed by police did not significantly change from 2017 to 2020, the *Times* took far greater interest in investigating deadly police violence the year when record numbers of people in the United States protested police brutality. The paper, proud of its investigative work in 2020, boasted, "Rarely has deadly police misconduct been so graphically revealed and documented as in the work last year of the Visual Investigations team at *The New York Times*."[62] It was as if the paper were finally discovering that victims of police violence were speaking the truth about being targeted on the basis of race.

And, admitting just how much power it has to influence life-and-death policies, the *Times* explained that its "videos either directly contradicted official accounts or revealed crucial details. Each helped trigger a national reckoning with a problem as old as the nation itself."

When a white pro-Trump mob attacked the US Capitol on January 6, 2021, Adeshina Emmanuel, writing for *Nieman Reports*, pointed out that "many journalists were quick to call out the double standard," of how police responded more gently to the January 6th riot versus the violence aimed at Black Lives Matter protests.[63] Now that journalists had been on the receiving end of police brutality, they could finally believe what Black people had been saying for generations about facing disproportionate police violence.

Emmanuel also concluded—perhaps too optimistically—that "the national uprising against police violence and anti-Blackness that followed has prompted a reckoning in newsrooms, many of which have audited their race coverage."[64]

It remains to be seen if newsrooms have moved beyond tokenism and buzzwords like "diversity" and "inclusion" to tangibly promoting racial justice narratives and restructuring the racial demographics of their editorial staff.

White (Supremacist) Newsrooms

In 1980, communities of color formed only about 20 percent of the US population. Twenty years later that number rose to 30 percent, and today, nearly 40 percent of the nation identifies as non-white.[65] This stunning demographic shift has not been matched in the newsrooms that tell our stories.

According to the *Columbia Journalism Review*, "less than 17 percent of newsroom staff at print and online publications, and only 13 percent of newspaper leadership" is comprised of racial and ethnic minorities.[66] The Women's Media Center found that women of color in particular make up "just 7.95 percent of US print newsroom staff, 12.6 percent of local TV news staff, and 6.2 percent of local radio staff."[67]

Rummana Hussain, a journalist at the *Chicago Sun-Times*, told the Women's Media Center, "Whether intentional or not, it seems like there is a cap on people of color in newsrooms."[68]

What's equally troubling is that journalists who analyze the media are largely white, and so fail to notice the problems within the journalistic landscape around race.

The Poynter Institute's Gabe Schneider explained that "the job of a media reporter or critic is to tell us about journalism's status quo, what's wrong with it, and what journalism could be if things were tweaked."[69] In his report on the lack of diversity among media critics, Schneider explained, "Media reporting and critique is a very homogeneously white space that often fails to bring a depth of personal perspective, care, and experience to these issues."

To summarize: newsrooms are mostly white, and those who critique journalism's problems are also mostly white, thereby failing to notice that white domination is a serious problem. While such manifestations of structural racism are categorically different from those on display at Fox News, both reinforce an unacceptable racist system that fails to uphold the humanity of people of color.

"Liberal" Media Begin Owning Up to Their Racism

In 2018, as Republicans' increasingly overt racism prompted more individuals and institutions to examine how things got this way, the revered journal *National Geographic* dissected its own racist past. Editor in chief Susan Goldberg wrote: "Some of what you find in our archives leaves you speechless, like a 1916 story about Australia. Underneath photos of two Aboriginal people, the caption reads: 'South Australian Blackfellows: These savages rank lowest in intelligence of all human beings.'"[70]

Goldberg admitted that her publication "did little to push its readers beyond the stereotypes ingrained in white American culture." Indeed, *National Geographic*, protected by its (undeserved) reputation for objective scientific curiosity, had, since its inception, promoted narratives that otherized people of color, Indigenous people, and tribal communities all over the world. "How we present race matters," she concluded, as she vowed to "prove we are better than this." She did not, however, apologize for her publication's promotion of racist narratives.

In December 2020, seven months after Floyd's murder, the *Kansas City Star*, a local paper based in Missouri, did actually apologize. After delving into its historic coverage through the lens of race, Mike Fannin, the paper's president and editor, wrote a piece titled "The truth in Black and white: An apology from The Kansas City Star," in which he explained how the paper "disenfranchised, ignored and scorned generations of

Black Kansas Citians," and how "decade after early decade it robbed an entire community of opportunity, dignity, justice and recognition."[71]

It was a brutally honest assessment that ran alongside a six-part series that the paper's own reporters created about past racist coverage. Fannin wrote: "It is well past time for an apology, acknowledging, as we do so, that the sins of our past still reverberate today.... Reporters were frequently sickened by what they found—decades of coverage that depicted Black Kansas Citians as criminals living in a crime-laden world. They felt shame at what was missing: the achievements, aspirations and milestones of an entire population routinely overlooked, as if Black people were invisible."

Importantly, Fannin also detailed numerous steps the *Kansas City Star* was taking to make amends for its racist coverage, including greater diversity in hiring, and the launching of investigative series examining police and gun violence, racism in the local fire department, and more.

In September 2020, the editorial board at the *Los Angeles Times* published its own mea culpa, reproducing some of its horrifically racist headlines and explaining how it had contributed to the dehumanization of people of color: "While the paper has done groundbreaking and important work highlighting the issues faced by communities of color, it has also often displayed at best a blind spot, at worst an outright hostility, for the city's nonwhite population, one both rooted and reflected in a shortage of Indigenous, Black, Latino, Asian and other people of color in its newsroom."[72]

In linking its racist coverage to the lack of diversity in its newsroom, the *LA Times* highlighted a critical problem in corporate news media outlets: how it pays lip service to racial equality but still structurally perpetuates white supremacy.

"On behalf of this institution, we apologize for The Times' history of racism," wrote the paper's editorial board. "We owe it to our readers to do better, and we vow to do so."[73]

While such apologies are steps in the right direction, it may be too soon to tell if media outlets like *National Geographic*, the *Kansas City Star*, and the *LA Times* have committed to improving their coverage of racial justice in the long term.

What's disheartening is that so few media outlets went even as far as admitting their wrongdoing. As I show in the next chapter, it falls to the independent press to compel corporate outlets to change their ways.

TWO INDEPENDENT MEDIA MAKERS ON THE FRONTLINES

GIVEN THAT RIGHT-WING MEDIA OUTLETS ARE PUSHING racist narratives to further their goals, and the so-called "liberal media" do too little, too late, to push back, it falls to the ranks of independent media outlets to create and promote counternarratives based on racial justice.

This is not a new phenomenon. Pacifica Radio, where I spent nearly two decades as a radio programmer, houses in its archive a rich library of recordings of civil rights leaders that are considered iconic heroes today, but who, during their lifetimes, were generally ignored or even vilified by the establishment press.

From talks by Dr. Martin Luther King Jr. and Rosa Parks to James Baldwin and Angela Davis, and almost everyone in between, Pacifica Radio's journalists painstakingly recorded speeches and interviews featuring movement leaders and activists of color considered too controversial for the white-dominated press. Meanwhile, their mainstream counterparts only found the courage to do the same decades later, after society had concluded that the Black Freedom movement was on the right side of history.

That trend continues today.

Believing Black Accounts of Injustice

On December 22, 2014, I invited Patrisse Cullors, co-founder of Black Lives Matter, for an interview on my live morning drive-time radio show on 90.7 FM KPFK in Los Angeles (also televised on Free Speech TV).[74] Together with her colleagues Alicia Garza and Opal Tometi, Cullors had helped to coin and popularize the hashtag "#BlackLivesMatter" in summer 2013, after the acquittal of George Zimmerman for the murder of Trayvon Martin in Florida.

Cullors, now a best-selling author and a sought-after speaker, at that time was not as well known to corporate media outlets and was rarely offered a platform to discuss ideas that corporate media outlets felt uncomfortable tackling.

She told me the origin story of the simple, but powerful phrase "Black Lives Matter" in the aftermath of Zimmerman's acquittal:

> I just lost it, I was crying and disturbed. We have all this evidence that this young man was hunted by George Zimmerman, and yet George Zimmerman still gets off the hook. So, what do our lives mean?... For me, it was this intense amount of grief that came over me. But I'm also an organizer, so I quickly moved my grief into action, and I just started going on social media and started writing [to] Black people and saying that I love them and checking on other Black people.
>
> Myself and Alicia Garza got into a Facebook conversation and she said this thing—to Black folks in particular who were saying, "We should have known better, of course they were gonna treat us this way"—she started saying to folks, "You know, I'm always going to be surprised. I'm never going to let them numb me from saying that our lives don't matter." And she said, "Our lives matter, Black lives matter."
>
> And then under the Facebook thread, I hashtagged "Black Lives Matter." And so, from there, literally in that moment, it was like a light bulb for so many Black people, and on social media at that point. And I started tagging Black folks saying,

"Your life matters, Black Lives Matter." I started tagging all my Black friends. I got on the phone with [Alicia] that night. We said we wanted this to be a project. And so, a couple of days later on July 15th, Riku Matsuda from *Flip the Script* here [on KPFK] called me up to be on the show and I was gonna talk about Black Lives Matter. It happened very organically.[75]

When I asked her if there was a link between the police killings of Black people and the history of Black people being lynched in America, Cullors said, "I think Black Lives Matter [activists]…are making those connections. And I think mainstream media is not talking about this."[76]

Although most news media in 2020 temporarily and superficially embraced the idea behind Black Lives Matter—the simple notion that Black people are human—they largely ignored it for the first seven years.[77] Luckily, in the meantime Cullors had a platform to speak about her crucial work: the independent press.

"If It Bleeds, It Leads"

Cullors had brought with her to the 2014 interview a young woman named Jasmine Richards, who had become newly politicized that summer when a white police officer named Darren Wilson killed a young Black teenager named Mike Brown in Ferguson, Missouri. Richards went on to lead a chapter of Black Lives Matter in Pasadena, California, where I live.

In what was one of her first live interviews, Richards made an astute observation about why protesters had engaged in property damage during the racial justice uprisings in Ferguson: "They weren't looting and messing up things to take them. They were burning things and messing things up so people could pay attention, so CNN could pay attention, 'cause that's the only way a Black life would matter, is if you mess up some stuff and go crazy.…What you see on TV is not really what it is."[78]

The idea that "if it bleeds, it leads" has long been a corporate media mantra, one that activists have taken note of. But independent journalists have generally refused to succumb to such pressures. Freed from the yoke of ratings and market valuations, independent journalists were able to explore and embrace the idea behind "Black Lives Matter" years before the corporate media caught on.

Similarly, independent media did not need to see videotaped proof of racist police brutality to understand that it was a systemic problem. In the era before smartphones, police claims ("he reached for his gun!") countered those of Black survivors, and corporate media readily accepted law enforcement's word. But independent media outlets, understanding the power dynamic between police and their victims, did not require proof of Black people's word. If Black folks said they experienced racist police brutality, that was reason enough to investigate and report.

Although there are exceptions, the narratives at work in independent media spaces have generally questioned authority and been mindful of Black people's humanity and truthfulness, whereas corporate media outlets have tended to reproduce an internalized narrative that police—and all other authorities—are almost always right.

Connecting the Dots to Build Racial Justice Narratives

Reluctant to connect dots and identify patterns in the public interest, corporate media outlets have often presented stories as if they are isolated incidents unconnected from one another. Malkia Devich-Cyril, founding director of MediaJustice, noted, "In stories about people of color, about Black people, in particular, the [media] coverage ends up being episodic versus thematic. History and context are lost in these stories."[79] For consumers of this type of programming, the political landscape can appear bewildering and overwhelming, best left to the "experts" to make sense of.

But context matters, especially in the case of Black Lives Matter. When presented in isolation, the phrase can appear jarring to those who enjoy white racial privilege. It can suggest that Black people are asserting their sovereign right to live in a way that's confrontational to notions of racial hierarchy. It should not have surprised us, then, that the defensive rejoinders of "All Lives Matter" and "Blue Lives Matter" emerged soon after #BlackLivesMatter was formulated.

When presented within the historical arc of racial violence facing Black America—tracing back to the barbarity of enslavement, the horrors of Jim Crow segregation, the systemic and institutional racist structures that persist—the meaning behind the phrase "Black Lives Matter" becomes crystal clear. Black Americans are demanding that the nation start valuing their lives, history, and rights, for it simply hasn't done so.

It is common practice within independent media to invoke history, to link seemingly disparate phenomena via common threads, to see the patterns that emerge and to be unafraid to craft narratives with long historical arcs. This is one aspect of what sets us apart from corporate media. And it is what helps readers and viewers of such media to make better sense of the world and its injustices.

In contrast, by reporting isolated stories with little background or historical framing, corporate media outlets rely on the internalized racist narratives promoted by right-wing media outlets to fill in the blanks for readers and viewers.

Rejecting Respectability Politics

Several months after her first appearance on my show, I invited Cullors back for a follow-up interview to discuss Bree Newsome, the fearless Black activist, musician, and artist who had just scaled a flagpole at the South Carolina state capitol and pulled down the Confederate flag.

I asked Cullors what she made of the fact that Newsome's actions had received widespread attention even in the corporate media, and how she was lionized as a model activist, with an impeccable educational background and well-educated parents. Cullors called Newsome a "local hero" whose powerful political statement was "one of the most creative, courageous actions we've seen thus far as part of the Black Lives Matter movement."[80]

But there is a downside to the media's focus on those activists who achieve celebrity status. "The media wants the perfect activist," said Cullors, "especially when it comes to Black folk." Newsome "has been idealized in a way, I think, she would reject as well," she added. What's heartening is that "this movement has been great at saying 'Respectability politics won't save you.'"[81]

The flip side of the corporate media's fixation on famous activists of color is the view that those who have anything but a perfect past are marked by their worst failings, and therefore deserving of whatever injustice society, police, the criminal justice system, or some other institution, deals them.

This is a direct outcome of white supremacy's dictate to subordinate and degrade people of color. When members of a racial group are presented as one-dimensional, the only dimension that inspires respect from elites is perfection. Any blemish is a deal-breaker.

People of color experience this routinely. We are constantly cognizant of the idea that a white supremacist society sees each one of us as a representation of our entire race. Any failing is a reflection on our community. This is rarely applied to white people.

"White people are seen as human beings," said Cullors, "whether they are LGBTQ, disabled, children, there is something about whiteness that allows for people to see them as full humans and people to have compassion about and empathy." Conversely, "when it comes to Black folk in particular, we're not offered that same compassion, we're not offered that same empathy."[82]

The "I" Word and Independent Media's Fight for Racial Justice

In the years following the September 11, 2001, attacks, right-wing media outlets routinely began referring to immigrants as "illegal aliens" or simply "illegals." Given the climate of fear and trauma that persisted after the attacks, such language went unchallenged and percolated into the rest of the corporate media. The federal government's technical term for immigrants, legal or not, is "alien," a word that literally invokes non-human beings.

In 2011, the independent online media outlet Colorlines.com published a lengthy investigation by Gabriel Thompson about how the word "illegal" was popularized by conservatives in order to pave the way for anti-immigrant legislation, and how mainstream outlets like the *New York Times*, along with Democratic Party leaders such as Senator Chuck Schumer, subsequently adopted the term. Thompson concluded that one consequence of this trend was "to move the political center ever rightward—and to turn the conversation about immigrants violently ugly."[83]

Race Forward: The Center for Racial Justice Innovation, which publishes Colorlines.com, launched a campaign following Thompson's investigation calling on the Associated Press to stop using the word "illegal."[84] The "Drop the I-Word" campaign pointed out that "casting immigrants as 'illegal' fuels dehumanization, criminalization, and anti-immigrant legislation across the country."

It took a year and a half, but in April 2013, Associated Press relented to the pressure campaign and published its Stylebook for the year explicitly excluding the word "illegal" to describe immigrants.[85] The AP Stylebook sets the standard for most corporate media. The decision to eliminate a dehumanizing word aimed at immigrants who are largely people of color was a tangible victory—one whose origin lay in an independent media operation.

Still, the damage was done. Instead of viewing undocumented individuals as people, it became easier to think of them as less than human after the words "illegal" or "illegal alien" had been attached to them over and over. In spite of several corporate media outlets agreeing to drop the dehumanizing phrase, right-wing forces had whipped up enough racist sentiment to pave the way for Donald Trump to win the presidency on an anti-immigrant platform just three years after AP's decision.

Rinku Sen, who at the time was the publisher of Colorlines.com, looked back on the campaign and noted, "Many of the national immigrants' rights groups just sat that [campaign] out. They didn't sign on," because "they thought that it would be a big distraction from the legislative fight." However, in a testament to the importance of using narrative to change policy, she explains, "The legislative fight didn't go anywhere because there wasn't enough narrative power, frankly, behind it, to make the legislation work."[86] Still, there had been a shift in journalistic policy such that when Trump took power in 2016, most corporate media outlets didn't repeat his dehumanizing language against immigrants.

Nearly a year after Trump lost his bid for reelection to the presidency in 2020, California Governor Gavin Newsom signed a bill replacing the word "alien" with "non-citizen" in all immigration-related state codes. The governor's office released a statement justifying this move because "the word 'alien' began to be used as a political dog whistle to express bigotry and hatred without using traditionally racist language."[87]

The story of how the word "illegal" was popularized and eventually shunned is testament not only to the power that language wields, but also to the importance of independent media in countering racist narratives. Building on such work are newer, more contemporary campaigns such as the Language Project, initiated by the Marshall Project in 2015 with the aim of convincing journalists to change the way they cover the criminal justice system.[88] Words such as "inmate" and "offender" obscure the personhood of those who are incarcerated. In contrast, referring to such people by name aims to dignify them, while underscoring the intolerable nature of the carceral system. In short, narrative-shifting with "people-first language" is a critical tool for changing public perception.

Right-wing media have perfected the art of relabeling concepts to push their agenda. If the so-called "liberal" media refuse on their own to aggressively push back and take a stand against dehumanizing language, conservatives win the day—except when progressive independent media outlets step in to shame the corporate media into doing the right thing.

"Your Accent Isn't Too Noticeable"

Throughout my journalism career, friends and relatives have asked me why I don't apply for anchor positions at places like CNN or MSNBC. It's a flattering and tempting notion to imagine reaching millions of people instead of a few thousand at the nonprofit radio and television stations that carry my show. But in my experience, there are very few avenues to break into the mainstream news industry for people who look and sound like me *and* who clearly state a commitment to social justice.

About ten years into my radio career, I briefly gave in to the temptation to believe that a mainstream newsroom might want a journalist like me and met with the program director of a local NPR affiliate station. I gave him a detailed proposal titled "Beyond Diversity," in which I asserted that "currently, white, male, higher-income, and older guest experts are overrepresented on KPCC and NPR programming."

In my proposal I made the case that "in order to expand its listening audience and better represent local communities, KPCC needs greater diversity among its guest experts, but also its hosts." I further explained that in order to attract more non-white listeners, the station would have to not only hire more programmers of color, but also shift its political leanings to reflect the more progressive views of communities of color. I promised that I would draw to the station my large Southern California audience of immigrant-heavy, progressive-leaning listeners.

The program director (who is no longer at the station) accepted my proposal and then mentioned in passing—almost as though he were paying me a compliment—that "your accent is not too noticeable" and therefore would not be jarring to listeners.

I never heard back from him.

I have found it is common practice on mainstream corporate broad-cast outlets such as NPR and CNN, or print outlets such as the *New York Times* and the *Washington Post*, that when journalists of color are hired, they often sound like, or write like, white journalists. This is not absolute. Admirable exceptions abound, but they are exceptions. KPCC's former program director openly worried that my accent might alienate listeners, but I suspect that he also worried that my political bent would do worse.

Perhaps if I had compromised my political views to align with those of mainstream journalists *and* adopted an American drawl, I might well have made it to a high-profile position at an A–list media corporation. With few exceptions, people of color only seem to make it to such positions if they curb their progressive leanings and non-white racial markers.

Bypassing the Gatekeepers

When I started my journalism career in 2002 at KPFK Pacifica radio, a low-budget, non-commercial community radio station in Los Angeles, no one made mention of my accent, my hard-to-pronounce name, my immigrant background, my gender, or my age.

The only test I had to pass in order to ensure that an inexperienced journalist like me could do the job of hosting a news show was…drum-roll…to prove that I could competently host a news show. After a few days of on-air trials, KPFK's interim general manager Steven Starr, who got his start at Indymedia, the Independent Media Center formed during the anti-globalization movement of the 1990s, hired me. He saw my race, ethnicity, and gender as assets to an independent media outlet like KPFK, not liabilities.

The United States has a rich history of independent media stepping in to do the journalistic work that established outlets fail to do and hir-ing people from marginalized communities. This is not to say that inde-pendent media always offer ideal anti-racist spaces where journalists of color are welcomed with open arms. As an insider I can safely say I have experienced my share of dysfunction—often, but not always, from white managers and fellow journalists fighting over scarce resources and occasionally replicating the problems faced by commercial newsrooms.

Still, even flawed independent media outlets do a better job than most corporate media outlets of serving the public interest and advancing a model of democracy based on universal standards of human rights, not the power of money. Moreover, those of us working within an independent media landscape have had the freedom to cover stories the way we want to, without the constraints of fitting our content around advertising, adhering to market research–based guidelines, or fearing backlash from elite conservatives.

In contrast, corporate newsrooms have many times more resources than independent media. Small armies of booking producers seek out and pre-interview well-known, eloquent guest experts for television interviews and arrange for them to appear physically or virtually for studio interviews. Content producers spend hours writing copy and preparing "talent" for the topic at hand.

The final products look and sound slick, polished, and at times even profound. But too often corporate media outlets fail to question the capitalist economy and racist system they serve. As a result, such media often refuse to acknowledge or challenge white supremacy and economic privilege.

Same Subject, Different Narratives

In media, it matters a great deal who is telling the stories. White media makers tend to reinforce narratives that preserve their racial privilege. Journalists of color, who personally feel the impacts of white supremacy, are more likely to offer counternarratives based on racial justice—especially when they are freed from commercial constraints.

Here is a stark example.

In early 2020, Howard Bryant, a senior writer for *ESPN The Magazine* and a sports correspondent for NPR's *Weekend Edition*, wrote a book called *Full Dissidence: Notes from an Uneven Playing Field*. Bryant, an African American member of the corporate media, opened his book with the words "To be black is to be a dissident."

His NPR colleague Scott Simon, who is white, in a brief six-minute interview skated across the surface of what Bryant's book was saying about white America being unable to accept Black Americans as full human beings. Simon even opened the conversation saying, "Much of the book is not about sports, but I do want to draw at your expertise in sports," almost as if he were warning Bryant to stick to what he knew best.[89]

Simon started the conversation with the subject of Colin Kaepernick—an appropriate opener considering how Kaepernick's story embodies the way America treats Black dissidents, and considering that Bryant focused on it in his book. But then, Simon spent much of the rest of the conversation on other well-known Black athletes—O. J. Simpson, Michael Jordan, and Tiger Woods—saying, "A lot of Americans thought their success and their popular adulation indicated America was over this race problem."[90]

"This race problem."

That a white reporter could so blithely dismiss the nation's sordid history of racist terror and current hostile climate is testament to NPR's own race problem. Still, in his answers to Simon's superficial questions, Bryant kept redirecting the conversation to what really mattered, saying, "What we see in the corporate world all the time, whether you're an athlete or not, [is] do you want diversity of color and diversity of thought, or simply diversity of color?" He added later in the conversation that "the minute [Black athletes] begin to embrace a political element of Blackness...we know what is going to happen to them."[91]

That's as far as the conversation went, and only those who purchased and read Bryant's book would eventually find out what he meant by the corporate world's rejection of Black Americans who criticize America.

A few weeks later I interviewed Bryant about his book on my own radio and television show.[92] Like Simon, I started with a question about Kaepernick, which he answered in a similar manner to his NPR interview, saying, "How much power do you really have if you lose everything for opening your mouth?"

I then followed up by noting that right-wing forces implied that Kaepernick was not patriotic, accused him of questioning the idea of America, and even denounced him as anti-military. This led us into a conversation—one that Bryant explored in an essay in his book—about the influence of the US military on the NFL and professional sports. Bryant told me that "this move toward military and toward defense is coming at an extremely high price. And that price is student debt."[93] He cited the fact that no one questions the $700-billion-a-year military budget, yet the question of how to pay for services like free college and free health care always comes up.

Together we explored a much deeper and broader terrain than the conversation led by NPR's Simon, with the same author about the same book. The interview was rich and textured. It questioned establishment talking points, upended assumptions, and explored the links between systemic issues.

For example, Bryant told me that there was a time when the US had a reputation for being "the place where you can go where you can aspire to the higher ideal, and that the flag represents that higher ideal." He then added, with brutal honesty, "But what I've recognized over the past few years is that the flag is something to be obeyed and not something to aspire to…if you don't obey it, you are now somehow less-than-American."[94]

We explored these profound ideas in roughly the same amount of time that Simon spent conversing with Bryant—about six minutes.

Unencumbered by commercial breaks—NPR likes to refer to them as "sponsorship messages"—and rigid formats, we went on to devote a total of nearly twenty-three minutes to the interview, exploring context, digging into the issues of democracy and social justice, and homing in on racist police brutality.

Bryant decried the assumption that "police are a force for good, when that's not the experience of the Black community or communities of color."[95] We touched on racial segregation in housing and education, prompting Bryant to ask, "Why don't we have better schools in our Black communities?"[96]

We examined the constraints on political speech, with Bryant saying, "We're being told to speak less, to say less about the military, to say less in sports, to say *less* about politics and not get involved in these things, at the same time when we really need to talk *more*."[97]

Indeed, NPR's interview embodied precisely what Bryant was criticizing. The narrow confines of Simon's vapid interview perfectly illustrated the author's claims about the limits of discourse in America. Instead of encapsulating Bryant's point for the audience, Simon exemplified it.

If Bryant, an NPR insider, could not get an honest, in-depth interview about his book on his own platform, what chance have other people of color who attempt to replace racist narratives with those based on racial justice?

Journalism by the People

When I began my broadcast journalism career, digital technology was just starting to enable cheaper, easier, and faster ways to document stories. I captured one of my first field reports on a portable DAT tape recorder, a compact device that hung from the shoulder. Soon, Sony's mini-disc recorders were all the rage, following which digital Zoom recorders were standard equipment for radio journalists. Video-recording devices took a similar turn, becoming more compact, higher quality, and less expensive.

Today, smartphones offer powerful means of creating high-quality audio and video recordings in ways we would not have imagined possible at the beginning of the century. Those seeking broadcast-quality recording devices need only spend a few hundred or thousand dollars to build sophisticated sound and television studios.

There are downsides to this digital revolution. Right-wing and white supremacist figures have used the same technology to terrifying effect, spewing racist disinformation and conspiracy theories all over the internet. But people of color, whether they consider themselves journalists or not, are telling their stories in powerful ways using the same means.

Taking advantage of this technological revolution, independent journalists now have much greater access to equipment, even when working for low-budget nonprofit outlets. And "citizen journalists" are bypassing traditional platforms and recording podcasts in stunning numbers about every topic imaginable. People of color are telling their stories, expressing their emancipatory aspirations, and reshaping narratives about who they are and what their vision for society is.

Freedom Dreams: Activists as Journalists

In the aftermath of the 2020 mass uprisings against racist police brutality, many media operations distorted or dismissed as unrealistic the specific demands by racial justice organizers to "defund the police"—a shorthand for diverting funding from massive police budgets toward education, true public safety, housing, health care, child and family support, and more.

The implied narrative behind the slogan is that far too large a piece of the pie is spent criminalizing communities of color instead of advancing them. Those who are targeted by the existing criminal justice system work to promote a social justice–based narrative critiquing what author Michelle Alexander calls "the new Jim Crow" and abolitionists such as Angela Y. Davis and Ruth Wilson Gilmore call the prison industrial complex. In contrast, those who have internalized the views promoted by corporate media and Hollywood—police are a necessary army in a war against crime and terrorism—see the idea of diverting the funds as an existential attack on public safety and security.

Casey Rocheteau, a communications manager at the advocacy organization Detroit Justice Center, says there is a "backlash in mainstream media," against defunding the police. "When people are calling the police, the police are telling people, 'We can't help you because we've been defunded,'" says Rocheteau.[98] Such an absurd claim, which a Seattle-based organizer shared with Rocheteau, was one reason why they helped to create a podcast called *Freedom Dreams* to set the record straight and promote racial justice narratives. In fact, neither Seattle nor Detroit police have been defunded.

"It's been important for us to think about not just what we're tearing down in terms of policing and jails and prisons, but also focusing on what we're building up," says Amanda Alexander, founder and executive director of the Detroit Justice Center and co-host of the podcast.[99]

Rocheteau and Alexander are using digital platforms to directly share with listeners the inspiring and under-covered stories of how racial justice organizers are challenging the way police budgets are determined, demanding an end to state violence, and advocating for a significant reduction in incarceration levels.

Coming at the issue of policing and mass incarceration from an abolitionist perspective that aims to dismantle carceral systems, *Freedom Dreams'* first episode spotlighted a grassroots effort to close the Atlanta City Jail in Georgia.[100] It was an inspiring story of how a coalition of formerly incarcerated women, transgender and queer organizers, and undocumented activists chipped away at the size of the jailed population, diminishing it from more than a thousand to just a few dozen.

The podcast's creators, feeling that the story had not gotten nearly as much attention as it deserved—especially in corporate media—spoke with organizers Marilynn Winn and Xochitl Bervera about their campaign to replace the jail with a center for wellness and freedom.

Alexander described her organization's communications strategy as "intentional" in "spotlighting the problems" and, more importantly, showcasing "the movement builders who are already resisting, that we can be learning from."

Not only have most corporate media reports of policing and incarceration missed stories such as the closing of Atlanta City Jail, but they also often present alternate narratives that do a disservice to communities most directly impacted by policing and mass incarceration, Rocheteau worries.

For example, mainstream media analysis of policing and mass incarceration often serves up dense facts informed by crime statistics and the complexities of city budgeting without relevant context about the impact on low-income communities of color—all while assuming that policing is the only way to tackle crime.

Rocheteau cited J. David Goodman's extensive report in the *New York Times* in October 2021 about the battle over police funding in Dallas, Texas. Goodman barely scratched the surface of what might be *causing* a crime spike in the city of 1.3 million residents, and he made no effort to examine why the abolition of police was a matter of racial justice. Instead, Goodman presented myriad statistics about how the numbers of homicides and police officers have changed over time.[101]

"Yes, it's important to know those statistics," says Rocheteau. "But presenting people with that information often leaves them in a position of feeling like 'What do I do about that?'"

With *Freedom Dreams*, Rocheteau and Alexander hope to inspire action by showcasing on their podcast the ways people across the country are engaged in abolition work. "In cities across the country, there is this move to say, 'We need to stop building jails, we need to understand why people are there,'" says Alexander. "We need to start meeting people's actual needs in other ways besides policing, and prosecuting, and jailing people."

Whether or not Rocheteau and Alexander are considered journalists in the traditional sense, they are using the tools of journalism to share the stories that mainstream corporate media fail to tell.

Such narrative work done by organizers ought to be considered part of the universe of independent media—especially when the goals are the same as those of the independent press: the elevation of human dignity through complex storytelling, the tearing down of narratives that fuel dehumanization, the building up of new narratives based on our humanity, and an end to oppressive systems.

THREE   WHITE HOLLYWOOD'S COPAGANDA

IN *BLACK LOOKS: RACE AND REPRESENTATION*, BELL HOOKS wrote, "From slavery on, white supremacists have recognized that control over images is central to the maintenance of any system of racial domination."[102] From the very beginning, the most powerful and well-funded American storytellers—the film and television industries—have systematically excluded non-white voices behind and in front of the camera. The industry, born in the siloed liberal enclaves of Southern California where I live, has a global reach. But its views often enforce white supremacist assumptions—particularly regarding police.

Many Americans have been indoctrinated to believe that police are central to public safety: if we want safer streets, safer schools, and safer communities, we must invest in law enforcement. That police are synonymous with safety is an underlying assumption of our city budgets, of mainstream political discourse—and of the plotlines of popular television programs and movies.

But there is no evidence that increased policing actually reduces violence. On the contrary. Most researchers and journalists attempt to correlate increased policing with a reduction in crime. But few ask whether increased policing reduces *violence*. A 2021 report by Community Resource Hub and Interrupting Criminalization called "Cops Don't Stop Violence: Combating Narratives Used to Defend Police

Instead of Defunding Them" examined numerous studies of police budgets and crime and found no significant drop in crime when police funding is increased. However, there are more incidents of police brutality, including fatal ones, where there are more police on city streets. The report's authors concluded that "instead of being violence preventers, cops are violence promoters."[103]

It has also been shown that police violence is disproportionately directed at people of color. A report by the Center for Policing Equity that studied thousands of police interactions found the average rate of police using force among Blacks to be "3.6 times as high as among whites, and 2.5 times as high as the overall rate."[104]

As I wrote this book, one of the most shocking incidents of police *inaction* to a violent fatal crime took place in Uvalde, Texas. When an eighteen-year-old gunman shot up an elementary school in May 2022, dozens of police officers waited for more than an hour outside a locked classroom where the shooter was firing AR-15 rifles at cowering children. One law enforcement official explained that police didn't break in because they were afraid, saying, "They could've been shot, they could've been killed."[105] Meanwhile, some parents climbed the school fence and rescued their own children in the face of police cowardice. Nineteen children and two teachers were killed in an incident that shocked the nation. A week later, the Poynter Institute for Media Studies published a report concluding that armed police do not prevent mass shootings in schools.[106]

The failure of police to intervene in cases like the Uvalde massacre, taken together with their constant propensity to fatally shoot unarmed people of color demonstrates that law enforcement is not about safety. The view of law enforcement held by heavily policed Black and Brown communities—almost entirely missing from Hollywood's fiction—is that policing is about enforcing racial hierarchy and the privileges it bestows.

White Writers Tell White Stories

Polls show that, regardless of income levels, white Americans feel safer around police and have a more favorable view of police than do Americans of color.[107] This is not surprising, given the racist nature of policing in the United States. It's no wonder then, that the white-dominated film and television industry perpetuates on-screen myths about police that are in line with white reality and at odds with what people of color experience. White writers and creators are telling the world *their* stories, and perpetuating narratives that reflect their worldviews. As acclaimed Nigerian writer Chimamanda Ngozi Adichie once said, "The single story creates stereotypes, and the problem with stereotypes is not that they are untrue, but that they are incomplete. They make the one story become the only story."[108]

Writers have a word for the vehicle they use to project their values onto viewers: protagonist. The protagonist of any well-told story is the fictional character that viewers are prompted to find relatable, whether it's a teenage superhero like Spiderman or a serial killer like Dexter. The most common protagonist in one of the most popular genres of television shows—scripted crime shows—is the police officer.

In reality, police wield violence disproportionately against people of color and usually avoid accountability with the help of a biased system of criminal justice, yet on-screen they are often portrayed as gritty, determined, brave, noble, seekers of justice.[109] When they falter, they are either justified in doing so, or pay a price for it.

The underlying narrative from television and Hollywood studios is that the institution that originated from "slave catchers" and that today continues to center on the violent control of Black and Brown bodies, is one that is honest, necessary, and legitimately powerful. When viewers internalize this view of police, they become blind to the history and ongoing racial injustices perpetrated by their real-life counterparts.

Human beings are natural storytellers—it is how we make sense of the world. Since the advent of moving pictures, we have become stunningly sophisticated in our ability to write, act out, and present realistic stories on-screen. Whether we admit it or not, films and television shows influence how we think about the world, and that, in turn, shapes our narratives on race to great effect.

As shown in this chapter, an enduring Hollywood narrative, especially on television, is the portrayal of police as arbiters of justice. For too long Hollywood has imbued fictional law enforcement officers with good intentions—by centering police perspectives, justifying the use of violence, and, most disturbingly, reversing roles of victim and perpetrator by routinely casting Black actors as on-screen cops.[110]

White Hollywood's Heroic Police

When the comic book–based TV show *Watchmen* was first released on HBO in late 2019, I thought the show held great potential. Based on a graphic novel series by the acclaimed writer Alan Moore, the show featured a diverse cast with several Black leads and developed a story line based on the 1921 Tulsa race massacre.

Excited as I had been to watch it, I was disappointed by the very first episode.

Showrunner Damon Lindelof, known for his sci-fi mystery thriller *Lost*, subverted the idea of masked crusaders by turning them into...police officers.

Policing is a central theme of the show, and cops are protagonists and antagonists. Early in *Watchmen*'s first episode, a Black officer pulls over a white man who he suspects is an armed and dangerous extremist, and when the cop is unable to access his firearm in time, the white motorist brutally shoots the Black officer. That scene, and its racial role reversal of victim and perpetrator, sets the tone for the rest of the show.

Several of the cops in *Watchmen* are portrayed by Black actors, chief among them Regina King, who plays the lead role of Angela Abar, a mask-wearing Tulsa police detective who is also a secret superhero named Sister Night. Lindelof's *Watchmen*, which received rave reviews and numerous awards, paints a world in which white supremacist vigilantes are out to get Black people *and* police. Those law enforcement professionals who are Black, like King's character, are doubly targeted.

It was a strange choice of tropes, to reimagine police alongside people of color as the targets of white supremacists. When asked about the central "superhero deconstruction story" of his show in an interview with *Entertainment Weekly*, Lindelof said, "I started to think that for *Watchmen*, maybe the more interesting point [than deconstructing the superhero] is to think about masking and authority and policing as an adjunct to superheroes."[111] In other words, police can be a version of superheroes in this make-believe world.

In an interview that aired on Sundance TV, Lindelof shared his long fascination with policing. "I grew up believing that Don Johnson from *Miami Vice* was a hero, a huge icon," he said. Johnson also plays a police officer on *Watchmen*. Referring to the two central law enforcement protagonists of the popular 1980s show, Lindelof continued, "There were story lines on *Miami Vice* where there were bad cops, but Crockett and Tubbs were not bad cops. They were never compromised." Still, Lindelof admitted this depiction was unrealistic, saying, "Oddly, they were living in some kind of post-racial Miami."[112]

The white showrunner also explained that one of the first TV serials he worked on was *Nash Bridges*, a show from the 1990s starring Johnson in the lead role of a San Francisco police officer. Lindelof recalled visiting San Francisco to do research for the show via "ride-alongs with the SFPD [San Francisco Police Department]."[113]

Whether Lindelof likes to admit it or not, he is part of a long tradition of Hollywood writers (usually white) who personally relate to and heroicize police officers and subsequently work hard to portray them in a positive light—an effort that some have aptly termed "copaganda."

Lindelof's *Watchmen* is a particularly sly example of copaganda, because it exposes audiences to the real-life historical tragedy of the Tulsa Race Massacre, casts a Black woman in a powerful lead role, and portrays at least some of the police officers as having questionable morality. But despite efforts to diversify the plot and cast, the series does not acknowledge the historically antagonistic role that police in the US have played in many Black communities. Leaving that dynamic unexamined and unchallenged only serves to uphold the racial hierarchy and injustice that still menaces much of the nation.

White Hollywood's Black Cops

Black actor Reggie VelJohnson is best known for his role as Sgt. Carl Winslow in the popular television show *Family Matters*. He has played a cop on-screen so many times over his four-decade career that some of his fans think he's one in real life. But in an interview with *US News and World Report*, the actor—who went out of his way to say he respects police—also admitted, "Cops make me nervous. I'm just being honest with you."[114]

It has become an increasingly common and perverse practice in Hollywood to cast Black people in the role of law enforcement—as if to undercut the reality of the constant threat that police pose to Black Americans in real life. But, as VelJohnson's experiences indicate, the ugly truth is that, no matter how hard Hollywood tries to whitewash police behavior by casting people of color as cops, in the real world, the mere presence of police is enough to inspire fear in many communities.

The role of Black police officer is such a popular one in television casting that *Essence* magazine in 2020 published a lengthy list titled "Our Favorite Black TV Cops."[115] Seve Chambers, writing about this trend in 2019 in *Black Art in America*, cited *Watchmen*, alongside numerous film and television projects of the time that showcased Black law enforcement characters, such as *Monsters and Men*, *Black and Blue*, *Blackkklansman*, and *21 Bridges*.

Chambers concluded that the portrayal of Black people in uniform was "strikingly, at an all-time high," and found it curious that Hollywood was engaging in such depictions, considering that the majority of high-profile cases of police brutality mostly involved white police officers brutalizing Black people. Chambers wrote that it was "something of a head scratcher that Hollywood chooses to view the matter [of policing] with Black officers."[116]

White Hollywood's White Victims

Toward the end of *Watchmen*'s first episode, Regina King's superhero persona, Sister Night, brutally attacks a member of a violent white supremacist group, clearly breaking the rules of policing that bind her to allow him due process. But, because a powerful Black woman is seen teaching such a vile white character a lesson, no matter how savagely, the audience can't help but cheer her on as she bloodies him. It is a sly way to get liberals who consider themselves anti-racist to celebrate police violence.

The advocacy group Color of Change in 2020 published "Normalizing Injustice," the first-ever study of its kind, covering scripted crime-themed television shows and how they "serve as a PR machine for the police."[117] The study, which examined in great detail twenty-six scripted crime shows across several top channels and streaming services, found that "across almost all series, wrongful actions specifically associated with racial bias—and prevalent in real life—were conspicuously absent with respect to depictions of [police] behavior." In other words, the world of scripted crime television is a post-racial world—just like the version of 1980s Miami that Lindelof remembers from *Miami Vice*.

The group's president, Rashad Robinson, writing in the foreword, quoted an order that some television writers receive from showrunners: "Viewers will change the channel if we make the crime victim Black, so you'll have to rewrite those characters and make them white instead."[118]

So, while in the real world white cops disproportionately brutalize Black people, in Hollywood writers' fantasies it's the Black cops who brutalize white people—as illustrated by the *Watchmen* scene of Sister Night beating up a white supremacist. Such fictional role reversal undermines the reality of racist police brutality and perpetuates a false narrative of the racial dynamic between violators and their victims.

Why does Hollywood seem so eager to cast people of color as police officers these days—other than perhaps to salvage the reputations of those who are increasingly seen as illegitimate authority figures? Perhaps because casting people of color as cops is an easy way to confer innocence and goodness onto those figures who in real life are responsible for disproportionately violating people of color.

Maya Williams, writing in BlackGirlNerds.com, said, "Hiring more Black cops did not stop the influx of deaths of Black people by law enforcement." It is similarly unsurprising that, as Williams's essay title states, "Casting Black people as cops will not stop Black people from dying."[119]

White Hollywood's Police Violence

In addition to increasingly flipping the racial script when it comes to the reality of policing, television and film often justify cops violating people's rights because they are pursuing justice for the greater good—a point again well illustrated by King's character in *Watchmen* when she violently brutalizes a white supremacist.

So prevalent is this theme of vigilante police that consumers of crime-themed television shows might conclude that violence is a common and necessary tool for achieving justice. The Color of Change study on "Normalizing Injustice" reported the situation specifically:

> Almost all series depicted bad behavior as being committed by good people, thereby framing bad actions as relatable, forgivable, acceptable and ultimately good. Remarkably, the data show that scripted crime series depicted "Good Guy" Criminal Justice Professionals committing wrongful actions far more than they depicted "Bad Guys" doing so. The likely result? Viewers feeling that those bad behaviors are actually not so bad, and are acceptable (even necessary) norms.[120]

Women of color—least likely to be portrayed as victims in crime-themed television shows, according to the study—are increasingly portrayed as police officers and therefore the perpetrators of violence—again, like King's character in *Watchmen*.

In spring 2019, NBC cast two women of color as the leads in a buddy-cop show called *L.A.'s Finest*. The duo, Syd and Nancy, played by Black actress Gabrielle Union and Latina actress Jessica Alba respectively, received poor reviews for trying, and failing, to re-create the typical on-screen chemistry of cop shows centering on male police partners. But, as one reviewer put it, "Syd and Nancy's primary skills as cops seem to be killing and maiming suspects without getting even a hair out of place."[121] So acceptable is illegal police violence on television that the reviewer did not even question the idea of cops "killing and maiming suspects" as morally wrong.

"Normalizing Injustice" notes that the "scripted crime genre influences the public to grant even more authority to police than they already have: to break the rules, to violate our rights, to cage the beast of crime as they would have us believe it is." Ultimately, the report concludes that "there is no stronger public relations force working against [police] reform than scripted television."[122]

Hollywood Didn't Always Love Cops

There was a time when Hollywood did not glorify policing. At the dawn of the movie industry, police officers were often portrayed as fools on-screen, providing comic relief, largely because of the contemporary view at the time that law enforcement was corrupt. In her history of pop culture's police portrayals, journalist Constance Grady traced how, within decades of the 1890 creation of the Lexow Commission, which uncovered extensive police corruption in New York, the movie industry in the 1910s mocked law enforcement in shows such as *Keystone Cops*, *Police Dog*, and *Easy Street*.[123]

A top police union, the International Association of Chiefs of Police, adopted a sternly worded resolution at the time denouncing police depictions and pointing out that "in moving pictures the police are sometimes made to appear ridiculous, and in view of the large number of young people, children, who attend these moving picture shows, it gives them an improper idea of the policeman."[124]

That began to change when the show *Dragnet* (1951) began portraying police in a favorable light. Not only did the show feature a heroic police officer as its protagonist, showrunner Jack Webb ensured that the Los Angeles Police Department's Public Information Division signed off on all his scripts. According to Grady, "Any element they disliked, he would scrap."[125]

Dragnet opened the floodgates of cop-themed shows, the most famous and beloved of them including *Law and Order*, *Columbo*, *Hawaii Five-O*, *Hill Street Blues*, *Starsky and Hutch*, and *Cagney and Lacey*. Scripted crime shows have been among the most popular genres of television in the United States and abroad.

As a teenager growing up in the Middle East, one of my favorite shows was *21 Jump Street*, a television series about a group of youthful-looking undercover cops who infiltrate a high school to solve crime. The telegenic actors glamorized policing to a generation of ardent teenage fans. Such shows have, for decades, shaped the minds of millions of viewers with a worldview deeply sympathetic to law enforcement.

In the months following the 2020 racial justice uprisings, some TV writers began finally grappling with how their police-themed shows were offering up fiction that was cut off from the lived realities of many Americans of color.[126] For example, writers for CBS's *MacGyver* (a new reboot of the old 1980s popular classic) began planning an episode in which the show's characters would tackle the issues of policing with a more nuanced view of race, and even hired consultants from a police reform group.

The Washington Post surmised that such a move could "repel prime-time viewers who prefer their police as full-on heroes."[127] The *Post* failed to understand or consider the millions of prime-time viewers who live in communities like Ferguson, Missouri, where police routinely prey upon people of color.

Notably, Patrick Lynch, president of the Police Benevolent Association of the City of New York, told the *Post* that such a trend toward more realistic police portrayals could result in "stories engineered to further diminish public opinion of police officers so that the anti-police movement can achieve their ultimate goal: the complete abolition of policing and total impunity for criminals."[128]

Lynch's hyperbolic sentiment is not unlike the resentment-filled resolution passed in 1910 by the aforementioned police union that felt police were ridiculed by on-screen portrayals. Luckily for him, Hollywood continues to promote fantasies of heroism among police in spite of some lip service to the contrary.

Hollywood's #WritersSoWhite

It's no secret that Hollywood has had trouble with racially representative writers' rooms. Darnell Hunt, dean of social sciences and professor of sociology and African American studies at the University of California, Los Angeles has tracked diversity in Hollywood for years. In 2017, Color of Change commissioned a report from Hunt to examine the lack of diversity in writers' rooms, examining all television episodes airing on eighteen platforms in the year before.[129]

Hunt spoke with me about the study's results, saying that "more than 90 percent of these rooms were led by a white showrunner." Additionally, nearly two-thirds of the hundreds of shows he examined "had no Black writers at all in the room" and "another 17 percent had only one 'token' Black writer."[130]

He found that "Blacks overall, made up less than 5 percent of the 3,817 writers that we looked at, across all the shows."[131] Such dismal numbers fuel the pro-police fantasies that play out in crime shows written by writers that have little real-world experience of being racially profiled by police or fear for their life in interactions with police.

Further, the "token" non-whites in the writers' room are outnumbered when it comes to crafting authentic story lines for shows. Hunt found that minority writers' complaints were strikingly similar, in that "it was a very alienating experience" to be in a white-dominated writers' room. "They felt like they had to prove themselves constantly, they felt like they couldn't bring up race, and if they did bring it up, they were often ostracized, marginalized," he says. Ultimately, Hunt concludes, "they felt often voiceless in these types of rooms."[132]

Hunt wrote in the report that where on-screen police portrayals are concerned, "none of the episodes acknowledged that Black people are routinely racially profiled in America or noted that police disproportionately brutalize unarmed Black suspects." Furthermore, he wrote that such episodes "routinely took for granted the legitimacy of the criminal justice system."[133] It's no wonder that for decades Hollywood's white-dominated writers' rooms have crafted a narrative so deeply at odds with the ugly reality of racist police brutality.

White Hollywood's War on People of Color

The 1973 Academy Awards offered an early glimpse of the racial tensions that existed in Hollywood's white-dominated industry. Sacheen Littlefeather attended the awards ceremony to accept Marlon Brando's Best Actor honor on his behalf. Her appearance stemmed from Brando's desire to draw attention to Hollywood's racist representations of Indigenous people.

Littlefeather, who identified herself as Native American, said in her speech that Brando was protesting "the treatment of American Indians today by the film industry and on television, in movie reruns and also with recent happenings at Wounded Knee."[134]

As she spoke quietly for barely a minute, the well-coiffed audience booed her, and only one or two individuals applauded. Offstage, the self-professed white supremacist actor John Wayne reportedly had to be physically restrained from rushing on stage toward her, apparently incensed at her remarks.[135]

Wayne was the epitome of Hollywood's idealization of white law enforcement, playing the heroic protagonist who faced countless "villains" of Indigenous ancestry in numerous films.[136] In a *Playboy* interview during which he labeled himself a white supremacist, Wayne said in reference to the settler colonialist theft of this nation, "I don't feel we did wrong in taking this great country away from them.... The Indians were selfishly trying to keep it for themselves."[137] He made those comments just two years before Littlefeather's speech.

Hollywood has spent years stereotyping Indigenous peoples. Indigenous men have been generally portrayed as "savages" and women as sexually available to white men. Older Native American characters are typically written as "wise shamans," "medicine men," or healers.[138]

On-screen stereotypes of Black people are just as horrifying. When they are not playing police officers brutalizing white victims, Black men are often cast as "thugs" and women as the "help" (literally, in the case of the film *The Help*) and/or the "sassy" or "angry" Black woman. Black men and women are also likely to be typecast as "the Black best friend" or the "Magical Negro," which is the Black counterpart to Native American shamans.[139]

Hollywood also stereotypes Chicanos/as, Mexicans, Puerto Ricans, and Latin Americans in general, in spite of the enormous racial, ethnic, and geographic diversity among them. Although the Latino/a community comprises nearly 19 percent of the United States, and is growing at a rate much faster than most ethnic and racial groups, Hollywood has routinely failed to represent them on-screen.[140] The 2021 "UCLA Diversity Report" found that Latina/o actors were given just 7.1 percent of all broadcast-television scripted show roles and 5.4 percent of film leads.[141] That's up from 5.3 percent and 4.6 percent, respectively, from the previous year, showing that although Latino/a representation is increasing, change is very slow.[142]

When Latina/o people are visible on-screen, they are more often than not horribly stereotyped—usually as members of violent drug cartels and gangs. Examples are TV series such as *El Chapo* and *Narcos*, and all the Latino roles in the popular dramas *Breaking Bad* and *Ozark*. Latina women are often portrayed, like the on-screen Indigenous stereotype, as sexually available, or like the on-screen Black stereotype, as domestic servants.

Asian American and Asian characters are similarly typecast. Men are often depicted as asexual, while women are sexually available—just like Indigenous women or Latinas. They are also often stereotyped as industrious, nerdy, or submissive, and are increasingly portrayed as the indispensable sidekicks of white protagonists. Often, Asian characters are stripped of verbal agency altogether, speaking little English or none at all, and are the butt of jokes rather than the agent. Classic examples are Hidetoshi Hasagawa in *The Office*, whose accent, when he speaks at all, is too thick to understand, or the almost entirely unspeaking characters of Annyong in *Arrested Development* and Brett in *Superstore*, whose tight-lipped personae become the punch lines of endless jokes.

Stereotypes specific to South Asians include caricatures with heavy singsong accents and poor social skills. Think Raj Koothrappali on *Big Bang Theory* or the Appu cartoon character in *The Simpsons*.

Hari Kondabolu, the stand-up comic, actor, filmmaker, and podcast host, in 2018 produced a documentary critiquing on-screen stereotypes of South Asians called *The Problem with Appu*. He says that as a child growing up in Queens, New York, he felt alienated by American pop culture: "You think you're American, you feel American…and yet you watch media and you're not represented. You don't exist as far as mainstream popular culture goes."[143] But creators like Kondabolu are now breaking into the industry. "It feels like there are old stories we weren't allowed to tell before that now we're allowed to tell, so it's almost like we're playing catch-up," he says.[144]

Americans of color in all our diversity yearn to see people who look and sound like us be portrayed as complex, multidimensional characters. Instead, we have for too long endured the indignities of watching Black and Brown people be misrepresented and underrepresented. It has been a long-term narrative assault.

The racist tropes served to condition audiences, normalizing degrading characterizations of Black, Brown, and Indigenous people faster than we could counter them. When media analysts refer to the "culture wars" waged against us by the right, they often fail to address the culture wars that so-called "liberal Hollywood" has inflicted against us for generations.

Nearly half a century after Sacheen Littlefeather called out Hollywood's racist narratives against Indigenous communities, she returned to the Academy Museum. In fall 2022, she was invited to be a distinguished guest of honor accepting a formal apology from the Academy of Motion Picture Arts and Sciences for the hostile reception she had faced at the 1973 Academy Awards. Upon reading Academy president David Rubin's words of contrition, Littlefeather told the *Hollywood Reporter*, "I never stood up onstage in 1973 for any kind of accolades. I only stood there because my ancestors were with me, and I spoke the truth."[145]

Remarking on the modest progress in on-screen racial representations, Littlefeather credited people of color rather than the Hollywood establishment, saying, "At long last, somebody is breaking down the doors."[146] (Weeks after her death, her sisters publicly revealed that Littlefeather fact did not, in fact, have the Indigenous heritage she claimed, and that she struggled with mental illness.[147] Still, her deception does not negate the claims she made about Hollywood's mistreatment of Indigenous people.) As I show in the next chapter, creators of color are fighting back in the culture wars that shape narratives about who they are, clawing their way into narrative-setting industries—and they are slowly but surely winning.

FOUR HOLLYWOOD'S CHANGING HUES

THE NARRATIVES THAT TELEVISION AND FILM PRODUCE influence how Americans perceive and relate to one another. But just as our screens can foster narratives that reinforce racial hierarchies, they can also be used to promote ones that dissolve them. We can, and should, think of television and movies as useful tools for narrative work and consciousness-shifting on a mass scale.

What's heartening is that that Black, Brown, and Indigenous creators are increasingly pushing their way into Hollywood in ways that are slowly, but surely, changing our culture.

Making Network Television More Black-ish

As shown in the previous chapter, television creators love crime shows that glorify police. Most commercial entertainment simply fails to portray racist police brutality and its impact on communities of color. But in 2016, an episode of the ABC sitcom *Black-ish* centered on the Johnsons—a fictitious Black family living in Southern California—as they watched news events unfold when a white police officer was acquitted for killing an unarmed Black man.[148] The adults in the Johnson family argued about how their children ought to interact with law enforcement, given that they are far more likely than non-Black children to face violence and even death in police encounters.

That *Black-ish* episode, titled "Hope," aired two years after the Ferguson uprisings. I watched it with my preteen son, who, receptive to issues around social justice, was excited and fascinated to see such a story for the first time as part of an entertaining TV show.

What set the entire eight-season comedy series apart from most other non-white network television shows was its intentionality. Marsai Martin, one of the *Black-ish* cast members, said in an interview with *USA Today*, "It wasn't only a sitcom, we would be hitting topics that not even dramas talk about." At the same time, "you were watching a Black family just live and be," she said.[149]

Black-ish creator Kenya Barris made no secret of his goal to bring issues of race to mainstream American audiences. The show's many political themes were testament to that goal. Covering vast terrain that included Black women's relationship with their hair, Black parents giving their children "the talk" on how to interact with police, the significance of Juneteeth, and even the legacy of the artist Prince, *Black-ish* was overt in its goal of educating non-Black audiences about Blackness in America, while also entertaining them.

It also, significantly, tackled broader issues such as divorce, teenagers' coming-of-age, nerd culture, and adults fitting in at work, insisting that its subjects were both uniquely Black *and* universally human. In doing so, *Black-ish* challenged TV's racist narratives about Black Americans.

Interestingly, the show was most popular among white audiences. For example, 58 percent of those who watched the show from September 2017 to May 2018 were white. Only 28 percent were Black, 8 percent Hispanic, and 4 percent Asian, prompting some critics to accuse Barris of making content tailored solely for white audiences.[150] Barris also faced criticism for showcasing a largely upper-middle-class view of Black families, which he countered by saying it was simply a reflection of his personal story.

In spite of some flaws, *Black-ish* made the case to network executives that shows with majority non-white casts that directly address racism and racist narratives can also be wildly popular. In doing so, it opened the door for other network TV shows by and about people of color. For example, as mentioned earlier, Nahnatchka Khan's 2015 *Fresh Off the Boat* centered on an Asian immigrant family in Florida; Sterlin Harjo and Taika Waititi in 2021 debuted *Reservation Dogs*, a dry comedy about a group of Native American youth in Oklahoma.[151] A year later, Ramy Youssef and Mo Amer debuted a Netflix comedy series about a Palestinian American in Houston navigating the asylum process; and Quinta Brunson's 2022 series *Abbott Elementary* won numerous awards for its portrayal of teachers at a majority Black public school.[152] All of these shows have enjoyed considerable critical acclaim.

Ultimately, the most effective racial justice narrative work in Hollywood must be done by those most deeply affected by racial injustice, as it is precisely their voices that are missing from mainstream culture.

Humanizing People Targeted by Police Brutality

Before he made the superhero blockbuster *Black Panther*, filmmaker Ryan Coogler released the feature-length film *Fruitvale Station*, a searing portrait of a real-life figure, a young Black man named Oscar Grant who was killed by a white police officer at the Fruitvale BART station in Oakland, California, on New Year's Day, 2009.[153] Coogler, who is a native of Oakland, cast Michael B. Jordan as Grant in the 2013 film. (Jordan went on to become famous for his role as Erik Killmonger in *Black Panther*.)[154]

Coogler shot the film in the style of a documentary, focusing largely on Grant's last day of life as he went about his daily routine: a morning cuddle with his girlfriend and daughter, a drive to the grocery store to buy crabs for his mother (played by Octavia Spencer), a quest to figure out how to pay rent, a stop at his mother's birthday party, and then, a final excursion to San Francisco with friends to celebrate the New Year.

In a radio interview about *Fruitvale Station*, Coogler told me, "My intention was to show who Oscar was to the people that knew him the best." He added, "So often in the media, young African American males are shown in very shallow ways…that aren't 360 degrees." Coogler was especially concerned that Black men, are "rarely shown in ways that are outside of being criminals."[155]

That is not to say that he wanted to portray only perfect characters—rather, he was interested in three-dimensional, complex ones. In *Fruitvale Station*, Coogler exposes viewers to a brief flashback from Grant's life a year earlier when he had been imprisoned, saying, "That flashback scene was about showing Oscar at his lowest point." Coogler's intention was to show what Grant's biggest fear was at the time, which was "going back to prison."[156]

Most notably, Coogler balanced his storytelling with the strong relationships that Grant had with numerous women in his life: his mother, his girlfriend, and his daughter. "When he was shot on that platform, you can hear on the footage, the first thing he said is, 'I got a daughter.' That was the most important person in his life," said Coogler. "In media representations of young Black males, you don't often see that side. They're kind of looked at as being these wayward characters who get girls pregnant, but they're not fathers," said Coogler. "Oscar"—like many others—"was a father."[157]

As the film progresses, anticipating Grant's inevitable end at the hands of police creates a palpable tension with each seemingly trivial moment in the last day of the young man's life, humanizing him and forcing viewers to confront the imminent loss of a man they could now imagine knowing intimately.

In choosing not to focus on the aftermath of the police killing, which became highly politicized and prompted mass protests, Coogler instead emphasizes the quiet complexity and depth of the life that was lost, refusing to let Oscar Grant become a mere statistic in the deadly and ongoing tally of racist police violence.

"There's thousands of Oscar Grants, there's thousands of young males losing their lives to senseless violence in our streets constantly," said Coogler, who was only twenty-seven years old when he made *Fruitvale Station*.[158] The film went on to win the Grand Jury Prize and the Audience Award at the Sundance Festival. It would be hard to imagine someone other than Coogler making the film—about a young Black man just like him, hailing from the same city, being attacked by cops in a neighborhood he was intimately familiar with. Hollywood's white creators were simply not capable of making such a film in 2013, nor were they, at that time, interested in projects that humanized the Black victims of police brutality.

Not Waiting for Hollywood's Validation

In 2011, I interviewed another Black filmmaker who was little known at the time and who would also go on to become a household name. Ava DuVernay was promoting her independent film *I Will Follow* as well as a nonprofit venture she had just launched to promote Black independent films.

Joining me at the studios of KPFK Pacifica Radio in Los Angeles, DuVernay explained that her work was a way to "present African American characters as we are: regular people who live and breathe and die and love, and do so in the way that everyone does."[159] She made *I Will Follow* in that vein, centering on a Black woman named Maye who packs up her deceased aunt's home and takes stock of her life. DuVernay drew from her own experiences to write the screenplay.

Reflecting on the challenges facing Black filmmakers at the time, DuVernay proudly explained that *I Will Follow* would have a theatrical release in multiple markets across the country: "This is the first time ever—ever, ever, ever—that a simultaneous national theatrical release has happened purely through grassroots means."[160] Lacking the massive marketing budgets of big production companies at the time, DuVernay had to rely on what she called the "passion and elbow grease" of a small army of supporters who used every means at their disposal—from

Facebook posts to leafleting to doing interviews on independent media outlets like KPFK—to promote the film.

When I asked her how much of a challenge it was for independent filmmakers of color like her to contend with an industry wary of projects without white, male leads, DuVernay responded presciently, saying, "We have masses of Black people who are starving for imagery. Why are we looking over there for them [white Hollywood] to validate and to give us permission to distribute our pictures?"[161]

She went on to explain, "I am not interested in pitching my films to studios, I am not interested in raising money with big corporations. I'm not interested in waiting for them to give me permission to distribute my images."[162]

Freeing herself from the constraints of mainstream Hollywood that would have her create projects designed to appeal primarily to white audiences, DuVernay found her footing in independent spaces and refused to compromise her vision. That approach eventually paid off.

A mere three and a half years after I spoke with her, DuVernay released the film that put her on the national and international filmmaking map: *Selma*, about a pivotal chapter in the life of Dr. Martin Luther King Jr. It was her first major studio film, and it went on to garner her a Best Picture nomination at the 2015 Academy Awards and more than $50 million in box office sales.[163]

In 2019, DuVernay explained the long and arduous road she had traveled to make it to that moment, including using up all her savings, bartering for film equipment, being denied numerous opportunities, and still persisting in an industry that for too long has excluded people of color.[164] Her organization, ARRAY, offers a model for filmmakers from other racial groups to do the same. ARRAY has gone on to release dozens of films by various Black filmmakers since *I Will Follow*.[165]

Growing numbers of Black filmmakers are now forcing their way into the national movie market. These artists demonstrate that creating for audiences of color matters. Where once only a handful of Black filmmakers, such as Spike Lee and John Singleton, could get major projects greenlit, today their ranks have increased to include DuVernay, Ryan Coogler, Jordan Peele, Boots Riley, Kasi Lemmons, Issa Rae, and many, many others.

While it's a good start, much work remains to be done to improve representation of Black people on-screen as well as that of Indigenous people, Latinos/as, and Asian Americans.

Inserting People of Color into Story Lines

Hollywood has, for years, excluded actors of color in spaces where their presence is considered anachronistic. For example, historical period dramas set in Western Europe have almost always had all-white casts. For that matter, even fantasy TV shows and movies like *Game of Thrones* and *Lord of the Rings* have, in the past, refused to cast people of color as anything other than monsters and villains, implying that this was in keeping with "realism"—meaning a white European fantasy.[166]

Things began to change in 2022 when new prequels to both of those popular franchises, *House of the Dragon* (HBO Max) and *Lord of the Rings: The Rings of Power* (Amazon Prime), featured Black and Brown characters with important speaking parts, and as heroic figures.[167] *House of Dragons* showrunner Ryan Condal said, "The world is very different now than it was 10 years ago when [*Game of Thrones*] all started. It's different than 20 years ago when Peter Jackson made *The Lord of the Rings*. These types of stories need to be more inclusive than they traditionally have been. It was very important…to create a show that was not another bunch of white people on the screen, just to put it very bluntly."[168]

Pioneering such incongruously diverse casting was the 2020 show *Bridgerton* by African American author, screenwriter, and producer Shonda Rhimes. Known for such long-running and popular dramas as *Grey's Anatomy* and *Scandal*, Rhimes executive produced *Bridgerton* as a television series for Netflix set in Regency-era England and aimed at Jane Austen fans of all races.[169]

Refusing to let historical accuracy dictate the racial backgrounds of the fictional characters, *Bridgerton* portrays royalty as polyracial, including lead characters of color. Its debut was so wildly popular that the show was renewed for a second season, in which Black actress Golda Rosheuvel reprised her role as the gloriously cool Queen Charlotte— alongside three new dark-chocolate-skinned female characters of South Asian descent.[170]

How do Black and Brown people make sense in the uniformly white world of Regency-era England? Simply by virtue of the creators' imagination and via a few clever, yet minor, explanations that serve as historical background.[171] Because, why not?

It's true that shows like *Bridgerton* ignore the oppressive systems of the time that subjected real-life Black and Brown people to violence and slavery. But, as Regina Gunapranata wrote in *Yes! Magazine*, "we shouldn't look to a period piece to inform us about racism—because it can't, at least not in a meaningful way. And that's OK."[172] *Bridgerton* visualizes how political power in a nineteenth-century British monarchy might manifest without racial hierarchy or domination.

While it is important that Hollywood not erase racist and oppressive structures of past eras, for people of color to see themselves in historical settings only as victims or survivors is exhausting and traumatic. We too deserve joyful entertainment in the form of on-screen narratives that celebrate our humor, romance, drama, fantasy, sensuality, and more.

Gunapranata added, "We need to see stories with BIPOC [Black and Indigenous people of color] protagonists experiencing love, joy, and pleasure. We need to practice worldbuilding, where we visualize the world that we want."[173] This, even in a work of historical fiction.

By inserting people of color where we don't expect to see them, Hollywood's increasingly bold creatives of color are rewriting the implicit narratives that live in people's heads about where Black and Brown people belong: which is everywhere.

Can Hollywood Craft Racial Justice Narratives?

In 2022, when Disney released a trailer for its new live-action version of *The Little Mermaid* featuring Black actress Halle Bailey as Ariel, there was an explosion of white supremacist vitriol over the racial casting choice.[174] One disgruntled person was so angry at a depiction of a fictitious being as Black that he edited the trailer video and replaced Bailey's face with that of a white woman.[175] Meanwhile, Black parents posted numerous videos of their daughters' overjoyed reactions at seeing themselves represented on-screen.[176]

The incident suggests that the mere inclusion of people of color on-screen—especially as protagonists—is still so rare that it can shift narratives about who belongs in our world, even when story lines aren't explicitly promoting racial justice. The exception to this is if the characters of color are used to whitewash racism or reproduce racial hierarchies.

As I noted in Chapter 3, many TV crime show writers have often sought to cast Black people as police officers in order to confer innocence onto characters whose real-life actions are often racist and violent. Award-winning Puerto Rican writer and musician Lin Manuel Miranda stands accused of doing something similar in his hit Broadway musical *Hamilton*, casting people of color as the nation's founders—many of whom were enslavers.

For years audiences have remained enthralled by *Hamilton*. The show earned rave reviews for retelling the story of American independence in a fresh manner, turning to clever hip-hop rhymes spouted by a non-white cast instead of the formulaic Sondheim-influenced format presented by mostly white actors.[177] In the early months of the coronavirus pandemic in 2020, when theater performances had come to a complete halt, the Disney+ channel released an all-star recorded performance of *Hamilton* in time for the July 4th holiday.[178]

But not all were delighted by *Hamilton*. Black poet and playwright Ishmael Reed wrote a scathing review of the musical, saying, "The producers of this profit hungry production...are using the slave's language: Rock and Roll, Rap and Hip Hop to romanticize the careers of kidnappers, and murderers."[179] Reed went on to write his own play, called *The Haunting of Lin-Manuel Miranda*, in which he expounded on his written critique.[180]

Stephanie Abraham, an Arab American author and pop-culture critic, also found fault with the show, explaining how *Hamilton* made gestures toward anti-racism without criticizing the white supremacy of the founding fathers themselves. She says that Miranda "wrote *Hamilton* as an abolitionist, as an anti-slavery advocate, and he wasn't."[181]

Telegenic Black actor Daveed Diggs was cast as Thomas Jefferson—a racist white enslaver, rapist, and arguably the most problematic of all founding fathers—creating a jarring experience for anyone familiar with Jefferson's background. Further, Abraham adds, "there's no recognition of Indigenous people on these lands at all."[182]

After *Hamilton*, Miranda's other Broadway play, the Tony Award–winning show *In The Heights*, was adapted as a film by the same name. Jon M. Chu directed the film—a story about a Latina/o community in Washington Heights, New York.[183] Although it boasted a majority Latino/a cast, some critics pointed out that Afro-Latinos/as were largely relegated to minor roles and extras in spite of Washington Heights being a predominantly Afro-Dominican neighborhood.

Afro–Puerto Rican writer Jasmine Haywood wrote in the news site Vox that while watching the film, she "immediately realized the racial composition of the light-skinned and white-passing Latinx cast was not reflective of what you see walking through that neighborhood."[184] Rosa Clemente, a Black Puerto Rican activist, journalist, scholar, and producer, also blasted the film, calling Miranda "anti-Black."[185]

Miranda is not the only one who stands accused of furthering racism and colorism in films with diverse casts. Clemente also pilloried acclaimed filmmaker Steven Spielberg for his remake of *West Side Story* in 2021. In a Twitter post Clemente wrote, "West Side Story was anti-Puerto Rican in 1961 and is anti-Puerto Rican in 2021."[186] She added, "Both the play and movies are racist and filled with racist tropes," and said, "This movie should have never been greenlit."[187]

Writer Rosa Cartagena agreed, writing in Bitch Media that the Spielberg film, which (predictably) received numerous Academy Award nominations, "reproduces the original film's artificial, unsatisfying portrayal of Boricuas while granting its white characters a chance for redemption in the eyes of a modern progressive audience."[188]

Clemente maintains that it *is* possible to showcase racial justice narratives in movies. She served as one of the associate producers on the film *Judas and the Black Messiah*, about Fred Hampton, chairman of the Illinois Black Panther Party.[189] The film, made by three Black filmmakers—Ryan Coogler, Shaka King, and Charles King—earned rave reviews for its nuanced and accurate portrayal of Hampton.[190] *The Guardian* newspaper praised actors Daniel Kaluuya and Lakeith Stanfield for their "award-worthy performances."[191]

"A lot of other Hollywood forces had tried to make this movie," says Clemente. She credits Charles King, "one of the few… Black executives in Hollywood," for shaping a film centered on the real story of how the Federal Bureau of Investigation infiltrated the Black Panthers in Chicago, destroyed lives, and tried to derail a movement for racial justice. [192]

From actors to executives, it takes creative people of color committed to racial justice involved in all aspects of film and television production to ensure that the narratives reaching the public are rooted in the humanity of Asian, Black, Brown, and Indigenous communities.

Pushing Back Against Hollywood's Cultural Appropriation

Another danger of simplistic on-screen diversity is that white-dominated Hollywood has often appropriated non-white culture. One example of this is Disney's 2013 effort to file a trademark application for the phrase

"Día de los Muertos," which was the original working title of the popular Day-of-the-Dead-themed animated film *Coco*.[193] "When we all found out, all the rabble, all the Raza, we went crazy," says Lalo Alcaraz, a well-known political cartoonist, writer, and film consultant.[194]

Alcaraz, who has remained rooted in his Mexican American culture and community, drew a scathing cartoon titled *Muerto Mouse* as part of the campaign to oppose the trademark.[195] He relates that "the Disney attorneys did not think twice about trademarking a community's religious and cultural observance.... They thought it was just part of doing business."

"In our country, every tradition, every celebration can become so commercialized that it loses its significance," worries Ofelia Esparza, an East Los Angeles–based master altar-maker whose cultivation of the art of Día de los Muertos earned her a prestigious fellowship in 2018 from the National Endowment for the Arts.[196]

Artists like Alcaraz and Esparza rightly fear that without their stewardship, corporations will appropriate and exploit their cultural traditions and rewrite the narratives that frame their history. When they and others pushed back and embarrassed Disney over the trademark application, the company quickly backed off.[197]

The filmmakers at Pixar eventually invited Alcaraz, Esparza, and other Chicano artists to be cultural consultants for *Coco* to influence the film's plotline and visuals.[198] Initially Alcaraz was suspicious, saying to them, "I'm not going to rubberstamp your project" and that he wanted no part of a film that would engage in what he called "Brown-facing," with white actors playing the roles of Mexican-origin characters.[199] He and other Chicano and Mexican consultants say they felt heard—which was especially meaningful in 2017, when *Coco* was released—at a time when Donald Trump was whipping up anti-Mexican and anti-immigrant xenophobia. Alcaraz told the *San Diego Union-Tribune*, "In political terms, this movie arrived at a perfect time to push back against all this hatred toward immigrants and Mexicans."[200]

Ultimately, the film's cast ended up being almost entirely Latino/a, a significant achievement for a community that is routinely under-represented on American screens.[201] "We needed that film to show Indigenous people, brown-skinned Mexican people on-screen. It's super important to show that," says Alcaraz.[202] Even if the end result was that Disney reaped large profits from *Coco*, the film brought authenticity and mainstream visibility for a community that Hollywood routinely stereotypes or renders invisible.

#OscarsSoWhite

Although Hollywood has finally begun to allow filmmakers and film consultants of color into its ranks, many still struggle to be seen and be treated as equals. In 2015, the year that *Selma* was nominated for Best Picture at the Academy Awards, DuVernay was surprisingly not nominated in the Best Director category. Actor David Oyewolo, who played Dr. Martin Luther King Jr. in the film, was similarly snubbed.[203]

Oyewolo and DuVernay later asserted that the Academy appeared to have punished the film in retaliation for *Selma*'s cast and crew appearing in T-shirts that sported police victim Eric Garner's last words, "I Can't Breathe," at the film's New York premiere. They based their assertion on a very revealing interview that the *Hollywood Reporter* published with an anonymous member of the Academy:

> When a movie about black people is good, members vote for it. But if the movie isn't that good, am I supposed to vote for it just because it has black people in it? I've got to tell you, having the cast show up in T-shirts saying "I can't breathe" [at the New York premiere]—I thought that stuff was offensive. Did they want to be known for making the best movie of the year or for stirring up shit?[204]

The shocking interview summed up the collective attitude of an institution whose members at the time were 94 percent white. It should not have been surprising that *all* the lead and supporting actors nominated in 2015 were white, and that all the directors nominated—with the exception of Mexican filmmaker Alejandro González Iñárritu—were also white.[205]

In response to the nearly all-white nominees, one observer, April Reign, posted a pithy tweet in 2015 that ended up sparking a movement to change the Academy's composition: "#OscarsSoWhite they asked to touch my hair."[206] Twitter users were soon chiming in with their own clever snipes at the homogenous hue of the Oscar nominations. The hashtag went viral.

It's easy to dismiss the Academy Awards as a superficial and increasingly unimportant institution. Indeed, the #OscarsSoWhite movement challenged the Academy to change or risk utter irrelevancy.[207] Still, for moviemakers, actors, and other industry insiders, winning an Oscar remains among the highest forms of critical affirmation.

A year after the hashtag was first popularized, the Academy, instead of doing better, shockingly offered a repeat performance, with yet another uniformly white set of nominees in 2016. Rage ensued, and Reign, who continued to be vocal in the movement, released a ten-point plan for change.[208] Interestingly, she didn't resort to a simplistic, nominate-more-people-of-color approach. Instead, her first exhortation to Hollywood was to ensure that film casts pass what she called the "DuVernay test," which was that "African Americans and other minorities have fully realized lives rather than serve as scenery in white stories."[209]

This was effectively a call to replace racist narratives with racial justice narratives on-screen.

Five years after Reign first posted her now-famous tweet, the *New York Times* concluded, perhaps a bit too optimistically, that "what began as a three-word hashtag forced an insular, $42 billion industry to change course."[210] In the years since #OscarsSoWhite went viral, the Academy's dynamics *have* begun to change, with members becoming more demographically representative of American society and the resulting nominations, consequently, more diverse.

DuVernay told the *Times* that the hashtag "was a catalyst for a conversation about what had really been a decades-long absence of diversity and inclusion."[211] While this represents an overdue transformation of Hollywood, racial equity still remains out of reach within this crucial narrative-setting industry.

In Fact, Diversity Sells

For years, Hollywood's mostly white executives claimed that the reason for movies and television shows featuring all-white or mostly white casts was purely financial and not at all racially motivated. But, as analyst Darnell Hunt has spent years saying, "diversity sells,"[212] in that time and again, movies and TV shows that have racially diverse casts tend to garner more ticket sales and higher ratings.

Hunt, who is dean of the Division of Social Sciences at UCLA and lead author of the annual "Hollywood Diversity Reports" on film and television, explains, "Films that look more like America's diversity, on average, have the highest box office [ratings]....Diverse films on average, are making more money."[213] The same logic applies to television: "There's a strong relationship between diversity in front of the camera and how well a TV show does in the ratings." He adds, "TV shows that look like America on average have the highest ratings."[214]

Just as media outlets have claimed that racist right-wing figures got airtime on radio and television because they generated profits, Hollywood film and television executives perpetuated the myth that no one wanted to see Black and Brown people as protagonists on-screen. It turns out such claims were never about economics. They were always about racism and racial exclusion.

Years of relentless activism from groups such as Color of Change, the Center for Cultural Power, Muslim Public Affairs Council, and National Hispanic Media Coalition, as well as grassroots pressure from the #OscarsSoWhite campaign, have pushed major production companies to start admitting creators and performers of color into their ranks. Not only are their projects performing financially as well as or better than those of their white counterparts, they are finally rewriting on-screen race-based narratives.

Actor Michael B. Jordan, partnering with Color of Change in summer 2020, launched an initiative called #ChangeHollywood to invest in content centering on racial justice.[215] Color of Change president Rashad Robinson said of this effort, "We know from our advocacy that the industry won't change on its own, so we're building off our current work to hold Hollywood accountable to provide a roadmap to enacting racial justice."[216]

But we can't rely on mass media and Hollywood alone to reshape narratives on race, and we don't need to be journalists or filmmakers in order to enact narrative change. As shown in the next two chapters, we all have the power to enact change.

FIVE   SOCIAL MEDIA AND COLLECTIVE POWER

WE CAN'T ALL BE JOURNALISTS, ACTORS, OR FILMMAKERS IN our quest to rewrite narratives on a national scale. But there are some basic tools—new and old—that we can all deploy to further racial justice. Today, individuals from silenced communities are doing just that, using digital technology and social media to assert themselves in collective ways, frame their stories, balance unequal power dynamics, and push back against racist narratives.

Chief among those leading the way are the increasing numbers of Black folks—collectively called Black Twitter—who are using social media to express their opinion on national issues. The Pew Research Center in December 2020 found that "social media platforms have served as venues for political engagement and social activism for many years, especially for Black Americans."[217] Digital platforms not only enable Black users to find like-minded people to connect with on matters of social justice, but, according to Pew Research, they serve as valuable tools "for holding powerful people accountable for their actions and giving a voice to underrepresented groups."[218]

Black Twitter is not an organized entity; rather, it is an organic collection of the unfiltered opinions of Black Americans on any number of topics, big and small, that has the unique ability to create trends. When it comes to serious issues like racist police brutality, in particular, Black

Twitter influences news agendas in ways that undermine the racist narratives that have historically skewed news coverage. Black Twitter draws attention to the persistence of systemic racism, distributes evidence supporting allegations of predation and harm, mobilizes masses of people to physically gather in protest, and offers a space to reflect and debate from a Black perspective. Black Twitter has become, in effect, a full-service reporting and mobilizing force that disrupts white supremacy while normalizing racial justice narratives on a national level.[219]

Before Black Twitter

Until portable video cameras became affordable to millions of Americans in the 1980s, when people of color described police violence in their communities, much of white America simply dismissed the allegations. Public access to camcorders and smartphones has changed that dynamic to some extent, although such devices remain pricey luxury items for many people. Prior to the internet, if a witness to police brutality happened to have a video recorder on hand to capture what they saw, they still had few options for publicizing their footage. Chief among those avenues was offering footage to news networks that were effectively gatekeepers, deciding whether or not to air the evidence.

Such was the technological landscape in 1991 when George Holliday, a white man living in the San Fernando Valley in Southern California, used his new Sony camcorder to tape from his apartment window the now-infamous police beating of a Black man named Rodney King in the street below.[220]

In the morning hours after he taped King being beaten, Holliday ran a marathon, attended a wedding, and then, more than twenty-four hours after the incident, he called the Los Angeles Police Department to inquire what had happened to the man. After an operator hung up on him, Holliday called his local TV station, KTLA, which subsequently expressed interest in the footage, then shared it with CNN.[221] As a result, millions of Americans witnessed for the first time what people in Black communities have been enduring for centuries.

Had Holliday not persisted in his effort to publicize the video via KTLA, or had KTLA not shown interest, or not shared the footage with CNN, the damning evidence of police violence might never have seen the light of day. It was the juxtaposition of Holliday's video with the acquittal of all the white officers involved in the beating a year later that sparked the historic 1992 uprisings in Los Angeles.

We'll never know how many incidents of racial terrorism and injustice have gone unreported over the years. Now, thanks to the internet and increasingly affordable technology, we need no longer rely on media gatekeepers in order to document and confront the violence of white supremacy in all its forms.

Darnella Frazier

Nearly thirty years after Holliday captured the footage of King's beating, a recording of another horrific incident of police abuse exploded into public consciousness in an entirely different manner. When Minneapolis police officer Derek Chauvin on May 25, 2020, bore down with all his body weight on George Floyd's neck for nine minutes, seventeen-year-old Darnella Frazier, a bystander, used her smartphone to videotape the entire fatal encounter and subsequently published it on Facebook in a post that went viral.[222]

She captioned the video of the brutal killing with two gut-wrenching lines: "They killed him right in front of cup foods over south on 38th and Chicago!! No type of sympathy 💔💔#POLICEBRUTALITY."[223]

Frazier expressed her response to Floyd's killing succinctly and effectively: She was heartbroken by the barbarity of what she witnessed, and she considered the police directly responsible for Floyd's death.

Frazier's Facebook post was the foundation upon which a national narrative emerged about the atrocity of Floyd's killing. The fact that it was posted swiftly and shared widely, without allowing time for news outlets, police, or politicians to establish their counternarrative about what happened, is central to the public outrage that Frazier's video footage catalyzed. Frazier enabled us to see what she saw, and feel what she felt, when Floyd took his last breath of life.

Frazier's role also highlighted the fact that Black social media users aren't just amplifying narratives about racial justice. They're also gathering irrefutable evidence of racism and publishing it directly online with accompanying narratives, without waiting for legacy media to make a judgment on what is considered newsworthy or reliable.

Months after Floyd's killing, Frazier's response to that horrific incident continued to inform public opinion. She took to the witness stand during the accused officer's trial and said, "When I look at George Floyd, I look at my dad, I look at my brother, my cousins, my uncles—because they are all Black. And I look at how that could have been one of them."[224] Frazier's narrative about Floyd was that he, like all Black men, was a human being, and his life had been wrongfully snuffed out.

On the first anniversary of Floyd's murder, Frazier wrote in an Instagram post, "Even though this was a traumatic life-changing experience for me, I'm proud of myself. If it weren't for my video, the world wouldn't have known the truth."[225] It was notable that the Pulitzer Prize board recognized Frazier with a special award for "highlighting the crucial role of citizens in journalists' quest for truth and justice."[226]

#Ferguson: A Turning Point for Black Twitter

Frazier's actions had a precedent—a situation that social scientists have closely studied. A few years before Floyd's killing, a Knight Foundation report on Black Twitter found that "participants often use Twitter to circulate and raise awareness about issues of concern on their own terms without waiting for professional journalists to take interest."[227] This is the direct result of low trust in the news media—an institution that, as noted in Chapter 1, has systematically excluded people of color. So, when a white officer killed a Black teenage boy named Mike Brown in Ferguson,

Missouri, in 2014,[228] Twitter users did not wait for legacy media to take note. Instead, they made Brown's killing newsworthy on their own.

Journalist Donovan X. Ramsey wrote in *The Atlantic*, "Witnesses to Brown's killing broke the news via social media. Within moments, their accounts of what happened spread through the Twittersphere with the hashtags #Ferguson and #MikeBrown."[229]

Northeastern University researchers Sarah Jackson and Brooke Foucault Welles took a closer look and examined half a million tweets posted in the days following Brown's killing that were hashtagged #Ferguson.[230] They found that within minutes of the shooting, a Black woman from Brown's neighborhood whose Twitter handle is @AyoMissDarkSkin had posted that the victim was "unarmed" and had been "executed" in the street. Her post was retweeted several thousand times before #Ferguson began trending nationally. According to Jackson, "How she tells the story in that tweet sets the tone for how the story is framed in many of the rest of the tweets about it."[231] Jackson added, "Twitter can allow everyday people who otherwise have little social or political power to shape a narrative about their experiences and what matters about those experiences."[232]

Instead of waiting for outside media to cover stories deemed to be important, Black Twitter creates content, deciding in an organic manner which stories deserve to be elevated. When stories get enough attention, this in turn often triggers news coverage at commercial outlets. The Knight Foundation report, which studied more than 44 million tweets in the period from 2015 to 2016, confirmed this, saying there existed "feedback loops in which a community created compelling Twitter content, media outlets covered it, and the community then circulated the media coverage of its own content."[233]

While Brown was one of thousands of people victimized by police in 2014, his killing took on greater significance after Black Twitter elevated the incident and made it a focal point for protest and traditional news coverage. The Center for Media & Social Impact (CMSI) at American University's School of Communication also studied millions of tweets in an effort to understand how Black Twitter users publicized instances of racist police brutality such as Brown's killing and elevated them as evidence of systematic injustice. According to CMSI, "Protesters and their supporters were generally able to circulate their own narratives on Twitter without relying on mainstream news outlets."[234] This is in marked contrast to the pre-internet era of white-dominated, media-controlled narratives around police killings of Black people, based on a knee-jerk trust in law enforcement.

But in recent years, Black Twitter's constituents have bypassed such framing with alternative narratives that are grounded in their personal experiences with police. And they have done so swiftly, collectively, and decisively, as in the case of the police killings of Brown, Floyd, and also Eric Garner, Freddie Gray, and numerous others. Indeed, the killings are rightfully seen as part of an ongoing history of violent white supremacy that reaches back to the days of settler colonialism. Among the most compelling counternarratives to the pro-police line, broadly framing these once seemingly disparate incidents of police violence, is the now popular racial justice slogan Black Lives Matter.

CMSI explains how, although the Black Lives Matter hashtag was first crafted by three Black women activists in 2013 after Trayvon Martin's killer was acquitted, it wasn't until the Ferguson protests a year later that the hashtag really took off—thanks to Black Twitter. "For more than a year, #Blacklivesmatter was only a hashtag, and not a very popular one: it was used in only 48 public tweets in June 2014 and in 398 tweets in July 2014. But by August 2014 that number had skyrocketed to 52,288, partly due to the slogan's frequent use in the context of the Ferguson protests."[235]

The CMSI report also quotes one thirty-year-old Twitter user named Brooke, who distilled the core message of the racial justice narratives she and others promoted: "#BlackLivesMatter is a very succinct and awesome way to acknowledge what we're trying to do…that people treat us like Black Lives Matter socially, politically. We are human and deserve to be treated as such."[236]

Black Twitter is also credited with creating and popularizing hashtags such as #ICantBreathe and #SayHerName to elevate the humanity of people of color victimized by police. It has become a remarkable narrative-setting institution—albeit a nontraditional one—built on platforms that simply did not exist a few decades ago, and that were not invented with such a transformative use in mind.

#MeToo

Black women, in particular, have used online digital technology to great effect, shaping narratives on race and successfully pioneering social justice movements. Social media has even helped to retroactively bolster Black women's historic leadership and narrative-shifting power, as in the case of activist and feminist leader Tarana Burke.[237]

When Hollywood's dirty secret of subjugating female actors to the will of powerful white men like Harvey Weinstein first became public,[238] it was a Black woman's hashtag, #MeToo, that effectively captured the widespread nature of misogynist sexual violence.

Although revelations became public in 2017 that Weinstein had, for years, raped, sexually assaulted, blackmailed, harassed, and subjugated women in Hollywood, Burke had crafted the hashtag #MeToo more than a decade earlier when she founded an organization to combat sexual violence against young Black girls and women of color.

In her 2021 book *Unbound: My Story of Liberation and the Birth of the Me Too Movement*, Burke explains that "back in 2005 when I started working on 'me too,' it was so difficult to get people on board."[239] Then, when actress Alyssa Milano remarked about the Weinstein scandal on social media, labeling her tweet #MeToo to illustrate the horrific ubiquity of sexual violence among women, Burke panicked, worrying that it would be appropriated by white women. She shared her concerns, saying: "Y'all know if these white women start using this hashtag, and it gets popular, they will never believe that a Black woman in her forties from the Bronx has been building a movement for the same purposes, using those exact words, for years now."[240]

Burke was in danger of being written out of the narrative around how the women-led movement against sexual violence was built—a phenomenon familiar to Black visionaries who have been the victims of cultural theft for generations.

"None of what was happening in Hollywood felt related to the work I had been entrenched in within my own community for so many years," she wrote of her initial reaction.[241] But Burke decided she would jump into the fray and pull out the "receipts" of her work so she could wrest back some control over the direction of the conversations. She posted a video on Instagram of herself giving a speech in 2014, wearing a T-shirt sporting the words "Me Too," and included a lengthy caption that said, in part, "The point of the work we've done over the last decade with the 'me too movement' is to let women, particularly young women of color know that they are not alone—it's a movement."[242]

At the same time, Black women on Twitter who were familiar with Burke's work chided white women to ensure that Burke wasn't written out of the narrative of the #MeToo movement. Since then, Burke has gone on to use the momentum from the Weinstein revelations to carry forward her work in the service of people who have survived sexual violence, recentering girls and women of color who have far less access to power and privilege than their white counterparts do. The social media landscape and its savvy users are making it possible for people of color to retain control of a narrative that centers them as social justice leaders and ensures they get credit for their work.

Art, Culture, and Digital Resistance

Social media are particularly conducive to the creation and promotion of artistic cultural trends. And while art may not be an obvious vehicle for shifting racial justice narratives, it has played a significant role in shaping cultural conversations around race.

Take educator Erynn Chambers, who identified herself on TikTok as "Loud, Bi, and Black af,"[243] and who recorded herself singing an impromptu song about policing and racism. The song, whose lyrics are short and sweet, and sung casually, went viral: "Black neighborhoods are overpoliced, so of course they have higher rates of crime. White perpetrators are undercharged, so of course they have lower rates of crime. And all of those stupid stats you keep using, are operating off a small sample size. So, shut up. Shut up, shut up, shut up, shut up, shut up."[244]

Chambers is one of many Black women using performance art, music, and other cultural forms to assert their humanity, share their opinions, and control the narratives about themselves and their communities.

Moya Bailey, assistant professor at Northeastern University and author of *Misogynoir Transformed: Black Women's Digital Resistance*, studies the phenomenon of Black social media users—particularly women—moving to the forefront of creative narrative-building in digital spaces.[245] In her book, Bailey singles out Janet Mock, a Black transgender woman and acclaimed Hollywood writer and director, who has helped to craft and promote racial justice and gender justice narratives throughout her career. Mock's hashtag #GirlsLikeUs is a prime example of what Bailey calls "digital resistance."[246] In 2012, years before US society had begun to acknowledge the humanity of transgender people—especially Black and Brown ones—Mock, who was trained as a journalist, tweeted, "#GirlsLikeUs is for ALL trans women, regardless of color, but all who lend their voice to amplify ours knows that intersectionality matters."[247]

The hashtag #GirlsLikeUs, according to Bailey, "created an opportunity for trans women to connect with one another, to challenge some of the stereotypes that exist, and create a network of communities."[248] The hashtag originated from the work that Mock did with young trans women who saw themselves as "just girls…with something extra."[249]

Mock used the hashtag to draw attention to the injustices facing transgender women and even critiqued the transphobic media coverage in the *New York Times* of the death of a transgender woman in 2012.[250]

After becoming prominent for her activism, Mock wrote a best-selling memoir and entered Hollywood to work on film and television. She eventually became a writer, director, and executive producer for an FX drama called *Pose* and went on to become the first openly transgender woman of color to sign a contract with a major media corporation, Netflix.[251]

In *Pose*, Mock brings to life the tight-knit communities of Black and Brown gay and transgender women and men who participated in the "ballroom culture" of the 1990s, who struggled with HIV and AIDS, and who created social structures to replace the family members who had rejected them. Although the series is marked by real-life tragedies, it is largely infused with joy.[252]

Only a Black transgender woman like Mock could have done justice to such a series. Further, it is hard to imagine the trajectory of Mock's career reaching the heights it has, without her unapologetic social media activism that started it all.

TikTok Dances and Cultural Appropriation

Young people of color are also using dance to shift race-based narratives online. Moya Bailey sees such art forms as part of the digital resistance she studies, saying, "One way that we can gauge how TikTok and some of these other platforms are being leveraged by minoritized populations, specifically Black women, is…seeing the viral successes of some of the dances that Black youth are doing, particularly Black girls."[253]

While it may be a stretch to consider TikTok dance routines as related to social and racial justice, in fact, the creation and proliferation of cultural trends is central to the humanity of the creators. And social media have allowed people of color to showcase their "receipts," if you will, to ensure they get credit for their intellectual and creative work. According to Bailey, young Black creatives on TikTok "are having to fight for their work to be connected to them."[254]

For example, in 2020, posts of young people performing an infectious dance called the Renegade were appearing all over social media platforms. Even the *New York Times* covered it, saying, "There's basically nothing bigger right now. Teenagers are doing the dance in the halls of high schools, at pep rallies and across the internet."[255] A fourteen-year-old Black girl named Jalaiah Harmon invented the dance. Like Burke, she worried that she would not get credit for it.

Harmon's concern was justified. Credit for the Renegade dance was largely going to white TikTok users such as Charli D'Amelio and Addison Rae, who had amassed millions of followers and have monetized Harmon's creation for their own benefit. But, because Harmon had public social media accounts documenting her creation—and because she asserted herself and called upon her own community of like-minded followers to help promote her work—eventually the *Times* and other media prominently covered Harmon, allowing her to tell her story and documenting her creative spirit and humanity.

White America has engaged in the theft of Black culture for generations. Now, social media engagement is helping to temper the thievery.

When comedian Jimmy Fallon invited Addison Rae on his show to teach him popular TikTok dances, he came under intense criticism for inviting a white dancer who was profiting off the creations of Black artists.[256]

Black Twitter had plenty to say about Fallon and Rae. One user, Noah Darden, said, "Y'all love using black people and black culture until it's time to give credit where it's due. #AddisonRae #JimmyFallon."[257]

The pressure built up, and although Fallon did not apologize, he felt compelled to invite the young Black creators of five of the dances on a follow-up show, saying, "We recognize that the creators of those dances deserve to have their own spotlight."[258]

Fallon was responding to the online power that communities of color have amassed to influence pop culture and push back against elites and celebrities when they engage in cultural theft or promote racist narratives. Had Fallon dug in his heels and refused to respond or to defend his actions, his show might have faced a decrease in viewership, and thus less potential advertising revenue.

Cancel Culture

When institutions and elites abuse their power, collective action through strikes, boycotts, and protests have historically been used to communicate demands. In the online realm, collective action from progressives to hold right-wing figures accountable has recently come to be known as "cancel culture." Lisa Nakamura, a University of Michigan professor, explained this highly politicized phrase to the *New York Times* in simple terms, saying, "It's a cultural boycott...an agreement not to amplify, signal boost, give money to. People talk about the attention economy—when you deprive someone of your attention, you're depriving them of a livelihood."[259]

An early target of cancel culture was Milo Yiannopoulos, the vocal alt-right activist whose 2017 speaking event at the University of California, Berkeley was called off after progressive activists launched an online campaign against his racist and anti-immigrant rhetoric. Yiannopoulos was subsequently disinvited even from right-wing gatherings and also lost a book deal.[260]

Another example is the openly white supremacist speaker Richard Spencer, whose speaking events at several universities were canceled after online campaigns were launched to oppose his bigotry.[261]

Sectors on the far right have been deeply resentful of activists' coordinated online actions against them, as have celebrities and other members of the elite who fuel racism, sexism, homophobia, and transphobia. Conservatives have railed against the dangers of "mob mentality," claiming they are being censored and their right to free speech infringed upon.[262]

The notion that "cancel culture" is dangerous has gained so much traction in national discourse that the *Wall Street Journal*'s Peggy Noonan denounced it as "a Leftist Offensive."[263] In addition, British actor John Cleese announced a documentary series called *Cancel Me*, based on interviews with people who have been "canceled."

The right's current fixation on cancel culture is part of an ongoing decades-long pushback against "political correctness." During his presidential campaign, Donald Trump said in 2015, "The big problem this country has is being politically correct." Trump's followers have gone on to rail against political correctness and cancel culture as an assertion of their right to free speech.

In reality, many of the cancellations are attempts to correct racist narratives. It's no wonder that many Republicans and white supremacists reject them. As Kali Holloway wrote in *The Nation*, "Conservatives' indignation is really just anger over the fact that marginalized folks—mostly thanks to social media—can now call them out for all the things they regularly say and do to further racist, sexist, homophobic, and transphobic agendas and white mob violence." She added, "What these put-upon conservatives are really pissed about isn't censorship or cancellation. It's consequences."[264]

It is also deeply ironic that white supremacists have engaged in the very behavior that they claim offends them. A case in point is the censure of football player Colin Kaepernick in retaliation for his taking a knee during the national anthem to protest police brutality.[265] Kaepernick's subsequent years-long struggle to sign an NFL contract is a measure of the right's success in ensuring he remains exiled from professional football.

Rigged Against People of Color

As much as online media provide a tool for the pursuit of justice, they are also used for purposes of disinformation. The price of having no gatekeepers is that false and hateful content has flourished online nearly as much as progressive work. Further, as many people of color have found, the algorithms of many popular platforms appear to amplify sensationalist and hateful content while penalizing those who call it out. The problem is so severe that Senator Ed Markey (D-MA) introduced a bill called the Algorithmic Justice and Online Platform Transparency Act of 2021 to tackle "discriminatory algorithmic processes caus[ing] disproportionate harm to populations that already experience marginalization."[266]

While prominent members of Black Twitter such as Mock, Burke, Reign, and others, remain active and have built large online followings, the fact is that most social media companies are run by billionaire elites, and are often rigged against people of color.

There are many examples of ways that platforms like Facebook, Twitter, and TikTok disproportionately police the speech of people of color while leaving white supremacist content online in the name of "free speech."

When researchers at Facebook in 2020 recommended that the company start flagging overtly racist speech, company executives decided to hold back for fear of alienating their "conservative partners."[267] One former Facebook manager, Tatenda Musapatike, who was disgusted by the company's position, told the *Washington Post* that it seemed as though "the health and safety of women of color on the platform is not as important as pleasing [Facebook's] rich White man friends."[268] As is the case with legacy media (newspapers, TV networks), a white-centric editorial framework is an unspoken part of the structure of most elite-owned businesses like Twitter, and profitability is simply an added bonus when it comes to enabling racist content.

Another example is that of the peer-reviewed health policy journal *Health Affairs*, which produced an exhaustive report on racism in the US healthcare system. When the journal attempted to publicize the report using paid ads on Google and Twitter, the platforms rejected their ads. Patti Sweet, the director of digital strategy at *Health Affairs*, wrote about this problem, "We know that search engine algorithms reinforce racism. But what happens when those algorithms mean we can't even talk about racism?"[269]

TikTok is also increasingly earning a reputation for being inhospitable to people of color. Black creators, per a *Los Angeles Times* report, feel "over-scrutinized and under-protected by the platform." Additionally, "users of color have complained that TikTok…handles their accounts and content in ways that seem unfair and racially biased."[270] Many users of color are noticing their content getting unfairly flagged and censored.

One TikTok user named Ziggi Tyler found that when he created an account on the platform's Creator Marketplace, the algorithm flagged as problematic specific phrases in his biography, including "Black lives matter," "supporting black people," "supporting black voices," and "supporting Black success."[271]

Confused, Tyler tested white supremacist labels like, "I am a neo nazi" and "I am an anti semetic" [sic] and found that the platform's algorithm considered such descriptions acceptable.[272] Though TikTok apologized and claimed it was an error, the company is making enough such "errors" that its algorithmic bias became the subject of an investigation published by the *MIT Technology Review*, which found that "those who are disproportionately targeted for abuse end up being algorithmically censored for speaking out about it."[273]

When racial justice uprisings were erupting across the nation in 2020, the powerful chief executives of tech monopolies—perhaps more accurately termed oligarchs—like Mark Zuckerberg of Facebook and Jack Dorsey of Twitter, declared their support for Black Lives Matter. But such declarations are undermined by the racist content that flourishes on their platforms and the unfair algorithms that subvert racial justice.[274] Black Twitter and similar communities have so far successfully engaged in social media activism to rewrite narratives despite the platforms being rigged against them. But that may change in the future.

There is an alternative for individuals engaged in shifting racist narratives, and that is person-to-person communication. As shown in the next and final chapter, there remains tremendous potential in old-school approaches to catalyze progressive transformation in people, in communities, and nationally.

SIX CHANGING NARRATIVES, ONE PERSON AT A TIME

THERE IS A DIFFERENCE BETWEEN TOP-DOWN NARRATIVE work such as that done by mass media, and bottom-up narrative work such as individual discourse, says Rinku Sen, executive director of Narrative Initiative. "We don't own Netflix, it's not a cooperative," she says. But "what we own is ourselves and our conversations."[275]

One of the most powerful ways we can engage in narrative-shifting is through individual discourse—a woefully underestimated form of interaction in these times when digital communication has turned many into passive consumers of ideas and opinions or combative foes cloaked in electronic anonymity.

Person-to-person narrative-shifting is—well—old-fashioned. But it often works. A prime example is the idea of teaching history in academic settings within ethnic studies courses or through the lens of what is called Critical Race Theory (CRT).[276] When the perspectives and cultures of communities of color are elevated, and when history is centered on justice rather than nationalism, it is hugely effective in changing minds about race and racism.

In January 2022, a white Republican college student named Brittany Murphree took a CRT course at the University of Mississippi Law School—despite her Republican friends and family members discouraging her from doing so. But Murphree was curious about the hotly debated approach to learning history and ultimately found that it transformed her thinking about race and racism.[277] At the same time, Mississippi's Republican lawmakers passed a bill banning CRT in K–12 schools and higher education,[278] prompting Murphree to declare, "The party I associate with just doesn't even know what the truth about this class is." She wrote a letter to her representatives, saying, "To date, this course has been the most impactful and enlightening course I have taken throughout my entire undergraduate career and graduate education at the State of Mississippi's flagship university."[279] It's no wonder that the far right has taken aim at CRT and ethnic studies, saying they promote biased thinking. Indeed, they *are* biased—toward justice and pluralism, and they have the potential to change the way young people think about race.

One of the most important and misunderstood aspects of US history that undergirds racist thinking is a whitewashing of the settler colonialist project that launched this nation. Studying the origins of the United States in a way that centers Indigenous and Black history is a useful starting point for exposing white supremacist influence in official narratives.

Dina Gilio-Whitaker, a columnist at the Indian Country Today Media Network and co-author with Roxanne Dunbar-Ortiz of the book *"All the Real Indians Died Off" and 20 Other Myths About Native Americans*, says, "I don't like the term 'Native American,' because it highlights the 'American' part of being Native and centralizes the part of being an American citizen." She proclaims, "That doesn't work for me."[280] Instead Gilio-Whitaker prefers the term "Indigenous peoples," and calls on us to use the names of tribal nations when possible.

Such a simple idea—identifying the people by their original national affiliation—strikes a blow to the myth of white people "discovering" the land now known as the United States of America. Indeed, it turns out that critical thinking about race in the US *is* simple—especially when one washes away the conditioning of a white supremacist education.

A Nation Born of Genocidal Settler Colonialism

For generations, Indigenous communities in the United States have protested Columbus Day—a centuries-old observance promoting a distorted narrative that glazes over the ways the original inhabitants of the continent were repeatedly betrayed, displaced, robbed, and massacred. Dr. Oriel María Siu calls Columbus Day "a transnational lie" that "must be undone because it becomes ingrained in [our] minds and in the ways in which children and adults understand who we are, where we are, and how it is that our societies exist."[281]

Siu, a writer and educator, has sought to recenter Indigenous narratives in children's books and in the classroom. She tells me that the myth of Columbus is "such a fundamental and important moment in history for all of us to understand and to know, and yet it gets taught in such a way as to continue to center and hero-ify white settler colonialism in the United States, the Americas, and abroad."[282] As a professor of ethnic studies in the United States for more than fourteen years, she says, "My 18- and 19-year-old students came into college classrooms with all these foundational 'fairy tales' as the base from which they understand the Americas, the place where they live and where they are born."[283]

Siu has found that many who take her classes—particularly white students—had internalized white supremacist narratives about Indigenous nations and other cultures. "White children grow up sheltered from understanding many of the realities and experiences of children of color. By the time they are eighteen or nineteen years old, going to college, they realize they've been lied to the entire time through their elementary and high school curricula," she says. "What do they do with that? It becomes a very important conversation in understanding how we can live in the same place through such different experiences for white and non-white children."[284]

Siu, like many academics of color, fought for ethnic studies courses to be taught in colleges and universities across the US to help educate students about the violence and racism often omitted in K–8 narratives of US history. She helped to establish the first Central American Studies Program at California State University, Northridge in 1999, and founded the Latina/o Studies program at the University of Puget Sound in 2012.[285]

Academics such as Siu have found great success ensuring that ethnic studies courses are taught in public colleges, universities, and even K–12 schools. California became the first state in the nation in October 2021 to require high schoolers to take ethnic studies courses in order to graduate.[286]

Researchers at the Stanford Graduate School of Education studied the impact of a ninth-grade ethnic studies class taught within the San Francisco Unified School District and found remarkable benefits. Students who took the course were more engaged in school, had better grades and attendance, and were more likely to graduate. The study's co-author, Emily Penner, concluded that "making school relevant and engaging to struggling students can really pay off."[287]

In attempting to understand why ethnic studies courses had such an effect, Penner speculated that "experiences where [students] grapple head-on with issues of identity and race and racism…does something to their level of engagement." She added, "That process is really useful to them in an academic sense, probably in a personal sense as well."[288]

Via such courses, educators of color have also been able to bring their own personal histories and experiences to white students who might otherwise not have had US history taught to them by those whose ancestors survived colonization, or who are the descendants of enslaved people, or who are first-, second-, and third-generation immigrants.

Siu finds that many of her students have a hard time initially accepting a woman of color as an authority on history:

> I've seen my own students having grown up with these big lies
> as their foundation for understanding the Americas. And at
> the beginning of the semester, they sit with their arms locked,

absolutely not accepting the fact that there is a woman of color in front of them who is a professor, and not wanting to engage with me. But once I begin to create a solid foundation, starting with pre-1492 history, and they begin to understand how it's related to everything—the environment, law, policies, health—their attitude tremendously changes and the questions they ask become different.[289]

This is precisely what higher education is meant to do—illuminate ideas via critical inquiry as a starting point for change.

Siu is also a children's book author, and her first book, *Rebeldita the Fearless*, centers on "a character who is born out of resistances, out of 529 years of Black, Brown, and Indigenous resistances in the Americas." Rebeldita is also "truly a product of the American experience. She knows that she lives on occupied lands and she wants to understand why and how."[290] Children's books like this one show that it's never too early to learn the true history of the Americas and to center racial justice narratives about the origins of the United States.

Critical Race Theory

Kimberlé Crenshaw, an African American law professor at University of California, Los Angeles first coined the term "critical race theory" (CRT) and co-edited a book of the same name, published in 1996, to define race as a social construct and provide a framework for understanding the way it shapes public policy.[291]

Crenshaw explained in a *New York Times* article that CRT, originally used by academics and social scientists to analyze educational inequities, "is a way of seeing, attending to, accounting for, tracing, and analyzing the ways that race is produced…the ways that racial inequality is facilitated, and the ways that our history has created these inequalities that now can be almost effortlessly reproduced unless we attend to the existence of these inequalities."[292]

Since Donald Trump's presidency, critical race theory and notions of "wokeness" have become a popular Republican target. Florida governor Ron DeSantis, among the most vocal leaders in his party, slammed CRT as equivalent to "teaching kids to hate their country and to hate each other" and claimed that "it ends up creating more divisions."[293] He also signed into law the state's House Bill 7, the "Individual Freedom Act," colloquially dubbed the "Stop WOKE Act," which penalizes educators and universities if they dare to pursue topics such as how racism infects the US Constitution.[294] The law also prohibits instruction that suggests an individual's "status as either privileged or oppressed is necessarily determined by his or her race, color, sex, or national origin," implying that there is no such thing as racial privilege or race-based oppression. (The law was immediately challenged on grounds that it violates the First Amendment.)[295]

History professor Robin D. G. Kelley is all too familiar with such attacks on critical thinking and education. Kelley, distinguished professor and Gary B. Nash Endowed Chair in US history at UCLA, explains that he "came into the profession at the height of a battleground over history, in the 1980s, with the war on political correctness." And although he lived through decades of conservative-led attacks, he describes the 2020s as "dangerous times," because now, "the right has far more political weapons. They are actually engaged in a kind of McCarthyite attack on schoolteachers, on students, on families, passing legislation to criminalize teaching Critical Race Theory."[296]

Kelley finds that conservatives don't even try to hide how racist their attacks are anymore. "Much of what's being attacked is very specific. It's an attack about race and gender and sexuality," he says. "There's a movement afoot to eliminate any education that actually reckons with the history of slavery, with Indigenous dispossession, with sexism and patriarchy."[297]

Opponents of critical race theory clearly feel threatened by the influence of racial justice narratives among young people. They claim they are simply part of a "grassroots" effort led by parents concerned about bias in their children's education.[298] But it turns out that secretive and powerful moneyed interests are actually fueling the war behind the scenes. In 2021, the watchdog group Open Secrets exposed the fact that right-wing organizations such as the Concord Fund are part of "a network of established dark money groups funded by secret donors…stoking the purportedly 'organic' anti-CRT sentiment."[299] Additionally, CNBC reporter Brian Schwartz has exposed the ways "business executives and wealthy Republican donors helped fund attacks" on critical race theory and that it is a centerpiece of the GOP's electoral campaigning.[300]

No More Happy Endings

Historian Yohuru Williams sees critical race theory as "a lens adopted by legal scholars that puts race at the center as a method of analysis for fundamentally asking about why, in spite of so much legislation in the 1960s, had there been no real substantive gains in conquering racial inequality in America." It's a good question. The legislation Williams referred to includes the Civil Rights Act of 1964 and the Voting Rights Act of 1965, neither of which fully undid the harms of systemic racism in spite of being monumental bills.[301]

Williams is a professor of history, the distinguished university chair and founding director of the Racial Justice Initiative at the University of St. Thomas, and the author of *Black Politics/White Power* and *Rethinking the Black Freedom Movement*. He explains that "the problem with Americans" is that we want "happy endings," and quotes William Dean Howells's famous advice to author Edith Wharton, early in her writing career, about the formula she should deploy for narrative arcs: "Recognize that the American public always wants a tragedy with a happy ending."[302]

According to Williams, "Our narrative is always: We were in this place and then some piece of legislation or some charismatic leader came along and we changed for the better."[303] In other words, injustices only exist in the past.

It's the reason why, in 2014, the Academy Awards rewarded the British-made film about American slavery *12 Years a Slave* with nine nominations. The film went on to win the Best Picture and Best Screenplay awards. Meanwhile, that same year, Oakland-based filmmaker Ryan Coogler was snubbed for his powerful film *Fruitvale Station* about Oscar Grant, a heartbreakingly honest portrayal of a Black man's final day of life before he was gunned down by a BART police officer.

Mikki Kendall, a writer for *The Guardian* newspaper, pop culture analyst, blogger, and creator of the popular Twitter feed #SolidarityIsForWhiteWomen, explains: "It's easier to think about the oppression of Black people in terms of slavery because that was then, and this is now. For the Academy it is very difficult for African-Americans to be telling a story about what African-Americans experience in America right now."[304]

The Academy chose to reward a film that, in the minds of its members, has a happy ending—slavery is over—and ignored one that points to the unhappy fact that police continue to kill Black people and get away with it.

Traditional American history education has trained us to have similar expectations. The result is the internalization of narratives that the United States was once deeply flawed on race but has now overcome those flaws. Such a perspective has helped ease white discomfort with the historical legacies of settler colonialism and the generations of displacement, domination, violence, and indignity inflicted upon Americans of color. Recentering racial justice narratives through educational methods like critical race theory can help the nation let go of whitewashed narratives with their confectionery "happy endings."

But what about those who are past the age of high school or college?

The Temptation to Cancel White Racists

A perfectly nice seventy-five-year-old white man living in the United States posted a meme to his Facebook page in 2018—during the peak of Donald Trump's presidency—sporting the words "I'm proud to be white. I bet no one passes this on because they are scared of be called a racist."[305] This grammatically incorrect sentence was superimposed on a Confederate flag and was reposted several times on this nice man's feed.

Elsewhere on his Facebook page was an image of President Obama with the words "Cuts Veterans Assistance by $3 billion, Allocates $5 billion for Syrian Refugees," and an image of a boy saluting the US flag, with the caption "Facebook had the NERVE to remove the beloved photo because non-Americans find it 'hateful.'"[306]

The fact-checking website Snopes.com debunked both assertions made in the graphics as false. But this man continued to post similarly inflammatory and easily refuted disinformation now common to MAGA Republicans. Such disinformation is often interspersed with cute videos and photos of animals and kids doing funny things.

Many, if not all of us know a person like this. He is one of millions of white Americans who do not consider themselves bigoted, yet reveal their inner feelings of racial resentment via memes and passing comments.

The United States was founded by white nationalists who structured the nation's institutions to dominate Indigenous communities, Black folks, Mexicans, Chinese people, and everyone but themselves. The fear of losing that racial dominance—and the real privileges it enforces—is what drives so many white Americans to embrace far-right politicians and media.

Do we write off these millions of Americans as hopelessly indoctrinated by racist disinformation? Or do we try to win them over and re-educate them?

German Lopez, writing for *Vox* in 2018, concluded that "accusations of racism can cause white Americans to become incredibly defensive—to the point that they might *reinforce* white supremacy."[307] This was the heart of Robin DiAngelo's bestselling book *White Fragility: Why It's So Hard for White People to Talk About Racism*.

While it can be extremely tempting to simply give up on dismantling white supremacy—*I* have, occasionally—doing so will not make it go away. The mission is daunting. But the visionaries who came before us, like Harriet Tubman or Fannie Lou Hamer, who risked their lives to fight for justice, faced higher mountains. Honoring their legacies calls on us to keep climbing, to continue rising up. So, even though there are countless Americans who have not had access to accurate history lessons in their K–12 education or college, who were not trained to think critically about the history of race in the US, or who have been indoctrinated by long-term exposure to right-wing disinformation—there is still hope.

Calling In Instead of Calling Out

Longtime activist and academic Loretta J. Ross has made it her mission to "build a culture that invites people in, instead of pushing them out." She does this by teaching a course she has named "Calling In the Calling Out Culture in the Age of Trump!"[308]

Ross has a long history of social justice activism that includes fighting against the Ku Klux Klan in the 1990s, co-founding the reproductive justice group SisterSong, writing three books on reproductive rights, and, most recently, teaching at Smith College as a visiting associate professor.

Ross is not as concerned about immediately transforming hardened white supremacists as she is interested in helping left-leaning folks realize how destructive some of their internalized racist narratives are to people of color. "In our pursuit of political purity, we're alienating a lot of our allies and we're criticizing them for not being 'woke' enough," says Ross. Her training is an important prerequisite for racial justice activists interested in doing narrative work to win over conservatives.

To help teach her course, Ross recruited movement organizer Loan Trần, who wrote a widely read essay in 2013, *Calling IN: A Less Disposable Way of Holding Each Other Accountable*.[309] Trần's article ignited a critical conversation about handling internal conflict within social justice spaces, which can be applied to conversations with people who may have internalized racist narratives.

Rather than calling out people for their offenses, Ross says, "I prefer 'calling in,' which is achieving accountability with grace, love, and respect as opposed to anger, shame, and humiliation," no matter how tempting it is to lash out at racists. She maintains that "the human rights movement is not a public therapy space. Its job is to end oppression."[310]

Ross offers a six-week online course that mirrors the college-level course she teaches at Smith College but costs a tiny fraction of the amount—part of an effort to make it as widely accessible as possible. Her goal, per the class description, is "building solidarity to take on White supremacy across different experiences in race, class, and gender."[311]

In addition to delving into ancient philosophies of conflict resolution such as Confucianism and Ubuntu, Ross's course explores the idea of "democratic speech environments" (DSEs) on college campuses, which were first envisioned by two scholars at Hampshire College. Christopher M. Tinson, associate professor of Africana studies and history, and Javiera Benavente, program director of the Ethics and the Common Good Project. The two authored an article explaining DSEs as "sites of justice-seeking conversation and discourse," which they hope "could be instrumental in shaping healthy and vital, rather than toxic and indifferent, campus climates." It's an approach that can be extrapolated outside the classroom.[312]

As an illustration of how people can talk to one another when someone makes an offensive statement, Ross suggests asking questions like "Can we practice when we're together, you not saying those kinds of things?" In using such an approach, she says, "you lead with love instead of anger."[313]

Agreeing to Disagree

The visionary writer and activist James Baldwin once said, "We can disagree and still love each other, unless your disagreement is rooted in my oppression and denial of my humanity, and right to exist."[314] I have often thought about this powerful sentiment and worn it as an armor to protect myself from racial trauma. But I come back again and again—perhaps because of an unfortunate optimism—to the idea that we can't give up on millions of people as hopelessly lost to racist narratives.

"Conflict is a part of life," says Nolan Higdon, a lecturer at Merrill College and in the education department at University of California, Santa Cruz. Higdon, who is an expert on digital culture, co-wrote a book with Mickey Huff called *Let's Agree to Disagree: A Critical Thinking Guide to Communication, Conflict Management, and Critical Media Literacy*.[315]

"Conflict, when addressed correctly can be constructive," says Higdon. "We know there are these hateful ideologies out there." But, he adds, "We're not asking people to get comfortable with a white supremacist" and their views. What he and Huff are advocating for instead is to take a "solutions-oriented" approach to conflict. "In a democracy, typically, the best ideas win the day when we engage in dialogue and try and change minds."[316]

He says people "are not born with" racist attitudes. These are "learned behaviors."

"What we're advocating is for people to figure out how to go about these conversations," says Higdon. According to him, there are certain conditions that must be met. First, "you can't begin to enter the process of constructive dialogue unless you have reciprocity." One example of this is for both parties to agree upon what sources of information are considered reliable. If people disagree on what constitutes a fact, there's little hope for dialogue.

Second, the venue for discussion is also important, and social media platforms are *not* appropriate for fostering constructive dialogue. In-person interactions in social settings are more conducive, instead, at family gatherings during the holidays, for instance.

Third, "rather than lampooning people or trying to own them, simply asking questions" can be effective, says Higdon. He offers the example of how conversing with a vaccine skeptic might be best met with questions like "Are you opposed to all vaccines, or are you just opposed to vaccine mandates?"

It turns out that such an approach has been scientifically tested and found to work rather well.

Deep Canvassing

While Robin DiAngelo's book *White Fragility* hints that there may be no hope for white people who have internalized racist narratives, new research on a technique called "deep canvassing" shows that it is indeed possible to change minds with one-on-one conversations.

In 2016, two social scientists undertook a promising study about ways to reduce or eradicate prejudice against transgender people. According to results published in the journal *Science*, David Broockman and Joshua Kalla found that "a single approximately 10-minute conversation encouraging actively taking the perspective of others can markedly reduce prejudice for at least 3 months." They recruited fifty-six "canvassers" to go door to door in Miami, Florida, and have ten-minute conversations about backing anti-discrimination legislation with voters on their doorsteps.[317]

The effects of the deep conversations created a positive change durable enough to move people to vote for laws protecting transgender people, even when they were exposed to counter-arguments. What's even more heartening is that the results were the same whether or not the canvassers were themselves transgender.

In 2020, the political activist organization People's Action partnered with the New Conversation Initiative and scientists Broockman and Kalla to see how effective such a method could be to change the minds of voters who were tempted to vote to reelect Trump.[318]

New Conversation Initiative explained that canvassers must aim to have conversations with two priorities:

Nonjudgmentally inviting a voter to open up about their real, conflicted feelings on an issue.

Sharing vulnerably about their own lives, and asking curious questions about the voter's life (especially the experiences that have shaped how they each feel about the issue).

As Congresswoman Alexandria Ocasio-Cortez (D-NY) has said, "The most powerful and persuasive things a person can say on any given issue is sharing their personal experience and personal story."[319]

According to New Conversation Initiative, "when we take this approach, people's experience leads them away from prejudice, stigma, or fear, and towards empathy and a willingness to consider progressive solutions."[320] The organization said deep canvassing is "the only tactic scientifically proven to be able to lastingly reduce prejudice, inoculate people against right-wing fear-messaging, and change hearts and minds on many of our society's toughest, most divisive issues."

Based on this, People's Action conducted what it called the "first-ever deep canvassing political persuasion experiment" to change voters' minds about Trump and found that it was "estimated to be 102 times more effective per person than the average presidential persuasion program."[321]

Brooke Adams, the director of Movement Politics at People's Action, explains that the program was "built to cut through the noise of the propaganda that people are hearing on *Fox News*," including "racist fear-driven messaging" and disinformation that "creates mass confusion."[322]

Instead of using slick approaches crafted by Washington, DC–based political strategists, Adams says People's Action trained canvassers on "how to listen, how to ask questions, how to engage with curiosity, and ultimately how to build a one-to-one relationship with people."[323] The results are surprisingly effective in helping people see their common humanity.

Although deep canvassing has yet to be applied specifically to racial justice narrative-changing efforts in an organized and large-scale manner, it offers a model for how anti-racist Americans can practice what they preach and work to promote racial justice narratives.

CONCLUSION RISING UP FOR OUR STORIES, OUR LIVES

ON JUNE 6, 2020, MY FAMILY AND I JOINED THOUSANDS OF people at a public park in Altadena, California, a small town near where I live, for a march and rally to protest the police killing of George Floyd. As we all sat on the grass quietly, the rally organizers called for eight minutes and forty-six seconds of silence to mark the time it took for Officer Derek Chauvin to murder him. A few moments in, Jasmine Richards, the founder of Black Lives Matter Pasadena, suddenly broke the silence, screaming out loud Floyd's last words:

Mama, I can't breathe.
Mama, I can't breathe.
Mama, I can't breathe.
Mama, I can't breathe.
Mama, I can't breathe.
Mama.
Mama.
Mama.
They're killing me.

A friend of mine—also coincidentally named Jasmine—was sitting nearby and joined this unrehearsed reenactment:

Help me!
Help me!

Help me!

Their screams overlapped in a cacophony of pain as soft sobs broke out across the gathering. Silence wasn't enough to convey the enormity of what had happened to Floyd—and to countless other victims of racist violence. Words were needed. And actions. The two Black women in our midst gave voice to Floyd's pain and made it their pain. And made it our pain. They rewrote the story of what happened in Minneapolis on May 25, 2020, transforming it from an isolated incident, into a narrative told with intention and truth, one that captured the stifling savagery of racism (*I can't breathe!*) and the demand for justice (*Help me!*).

We are a long way from attaining racial justice, or even ending police brutality. We are a long way from equity in housing, employment, education, health care, and wealth. But we are in movement together—organizing, speaking out, rising up together.

Our nation is experiencing a profound, albeit messy, evolution. What has been a centuries-long white nationalist project based on the displacement of Indigenous people and funded by the enslavement of people snatched from Africa, is today rapidly transforming into a multihued state. The good news is that people of color are broadcasting our stories, and reshaping cultural narratives about who we are, as never before. The 2022 *Hollywood Diversity Report* found that although Black Americans comprise 13.4 percent of the US population, their share of film leads in the year 2021 was 15.5 percent.[324] Although this was a drop from 19 percent the year before, the fact that Black leads remain overrepresented in film is a stunning testament to Black filmmakers and creators who have clawed their way into Hollywood's executive suites and ensured that the stories of their people, their families, and their communities are told in gloriously complex and nuanced ways for the rest of the nation and the world to see.[325] Increasing representation for Latinos/as, Asians, and Indigenous people to arrive at parity with their populations remains a work in progress.

The bad news is, the laws and norms of the nation haven't caught up to this increased racial diversity. The white nationalist legacies of settler colonialism persist. Voting rights have been rolled back in ways that aim to delay the coming extinction of these legacies. The criminal justice system remains racist. Law enforcement continues to operate with impunity, sucking up resources from our cities in order to disproportionately criminalize people of color and even kill us. Health outcomes remain skewed by race. Low-paying jobs are concentrated in communities of color. Neighborhoods and public schools remain racially segregated. Armed white supremacist militias and vigilantes target those deemed to be "other." Political decision-making, wealth, and leadership roles in government, finance, and major institutions remain in the tight grip of white elites.

It's no wonder there's a violent tension that is roiling society as power remains rigidly hoarded and systemic racism continues to infect us. As Dr. Cornel West said in 2020, "You either have the kind of nonviolent revolution that takes the form of the democratic sharing of wealth, power, resources and dignity—or, you end up with a White backlash that is so vicious that it cannot but lead toward authoritarian regime.... We don't know which way this thing is going to go. It's a fork in the road."[326]

Envisioning the world we want through narrative-shifting is a crucial step in changing our relationships with power and one another. Political organizing is also a critical part of the process, but it's not enough on its own. All of these are necessary for transforming the consciousness and material conditions of the nation.

Narrative Work on Its Own Is PR

Storytelling alone does not change the world. The great abolitionist leader Frederick Douglass said in an 1857 speech, "Power concedes nothing without a demand. It never did and it never will."[327] Replacing racist narratives with those based on racial justice—stories rooted in our humanity—is one essential element of the long road to redistributing power. As people of color have inserted themselves into narrative-setting industries to rewrite their stories, corporate America and government agencies have begun to embrace the *idea* of racial justice—but not necessarily the long-term policy changes required to realize that idea. The danger of narrative-shifting is that, in isolation, it can be co-opted for public relations and marketing by powerful institutions.

For example, after the lynching of George Floyd and the mass racial justice uprising that it sparked, corporate America embraced the slogan "Black Lives Matter." Companies realized it was good public relations to affirm the humanity of Black people. According to the *Washington Post*, after the uprisings of 2020, the nation's fifty biggest corporations and their allied foundations pledged $50 billion to address racial inequality.[328]

But of that amount, only about $70 million was donated via grants to criminal justice reform organizations. Ninety percent of the funds have been allocated to "loans or investments" that the companies "could stand to profit from, more than half in the form of mortgages." The *Post* conceded that "profit-driven corporations will not propel transformational change with money alone, experts say."[329] In other words, racial justice narratives will be used for marketing ploys unless corporate executives are pushed to comply with laws that promote racial equity.

Similarly, President Joe Biden's administration adopted the language of racial justice, announcing an executive order in January 2021 on "Advancing Racial Equity and Support for Underserved Communities Through the Federal Government."[330] While the order is a noble undertaking and was the direct result of grassroots racial justice organizing, as of this writing its goals remain unattained. Producing such orders allows the Biden administration to claim the mantle of anti-racism without actually engaging in the work of making government a force for racial justice.

Incorporating Narrative Work into Organizing

Today, social justice organizations and movements are increasingly incorporating narrative work into their arsenal of organizing tools.

There are numerous organizations led by people of color that promote such work, including RadComms (short for Radical Communicators Network); ReFrame, which says it "builds narrative power to win"; and a 2016 effort called Narrative Initiative that declares the goal to "equip leaders with the knowledge and skills necessary to harness the power of narrative for social change." The initiative's executive director, Rinku Sen, says she is "trying to build narrative power" and that it is critical to understand that it matters who has the power to create and promote narratives. "We're all making narrative all the time," says Sen, adding, "I just want people to be deliberate about that."[331]

For example, the Coalition for Humane Immigrant Rights in Los Angeles (CHIRLA), which has worked since 1986 to win protections and rights for immigrants, has embraced narrative work explicitly. Because immigrants are rarely portrayed in Hollywood film or television projects except as caricatures and stereotypes, the human cost of our harsh immigration policies remains under-portrayed in film, despite the harm that countless people face. To remedy that, in 2022 CHIRLA backed the production of a feature film—*America's Family*—that was directed, written, and produced by a Black woman named Anike Tourse.[332]

The film centers on a mixed-status family in the US whose members face detention and deportation. CHIRLA's executive director, Angelica Salas, says that "the stories of immigrants are rarely told by immigrants," and so this film "was created in order to tell our story from our perspective, from an immigrant lens."[333]

This sort of narrative work can be part of a core strategy for achieving social transformation, political change, and a balance of power commensurate with demographic realities. Salas explains, "We see this film as a tool toward our policy and advocacy goal, which is to change our immigration laws so that they are more just and more humane and so that they keep our families together. That is its purpose." Salas also hopes the film simply humanizes immigrants, saying she wants it "to connect with a broader American audience, to really show what's happening to [immigrant] families and to really connect them to their own families."[334]

Making a film is quite different from putting out a press release; CHIRLA does both. "There is a difference between doing narrative strategy and doing strategic communications," says Sen. The latter is "usually short term [six months to a year] and usually tied to a policy outcome that we want," she explains. But "the time lines we're operating on in shifting narrative are more like thirty, forty, fifty years."[335] In other words, narrative work takes time and patience, and is meant to last.

Such change, in Sen's view, amounts to "a shift in the values that matter most to people and a shift in norms—'this is acceptable to talk about, this is not'—and a shift in actions, like what institutions and individuals feel like they're supposed to do to be part of the community or the country."[336]

Organizing for racial justice becomes easier in a world where people of color are engaged in spirited journalism to uncover injustices, create worlds on-screen that reflect the justice we are due, and connect with fellow Americans about who we are and what we deserve.

Frustration and Hope

This book was born out of decades of frustration. Working as an independent journalist unfettered by the demands of commercial media, I was perpetually exasperated by the built-in slants of my corporate counterparts. That exasperation gave me the clarity to understand how traditional news media and their internalized white supremacist frameworks have shaped public opinion.

The stories and perspectives we see in the media have indeed changed for the better. Commitments to incorporate principles of diversity, equity, and inclusion into media workplaces are an improvement over an earlier era wedded to the belief that white journalists could impartially cover stories that impact people of color.

Although they are more diverse than before, corporate newsrooms' legacy of white domination persists. According to Pew Research, 77 percent of newsroom employees are white, while only about 61 percent of the population is white.[337] And, above all, media's top corporate leadership remains dominated by whites. The media reform organization Free Press concluded that "companies led by White men own nearly all of our media."[338]

It's not enough to hire a sole Black journalist and assign them coverage of MLK Day, or send the only Latina/o journalist in the newsroom to cover all immigration stories. It's particularly galling when journalists of color are expected to function as "race ombudsmen" and help keep their institutions accountable on matters of race. Narrative-shifting is a work in progress. Much still needs to be done to dismantle racism in news media, and journalists of color remain overburdened with the task.

We need to do much better. We need equity in the newsroom and in how our stories are covered. This means a transformation in the racial makeup of news media leadership. It means ensuring that newsrooms properly reflect diverse communities and demonstrate a commitment to racial justice. It means accountability—including apology and even reparations for centuries of racist media coverage. It means strong financial support—not from philanthropic institutions, which often comes with the organization's own set of strings attached—but via government support for noncommercial journalism done in the public interest.

This book was also born out of decades of hope. When I first moved to the greater Los Angeles area in 1998, I braced myself for the superficiality of Hollywood, the excesses of Beverly Hills, the brutality of the Los Angeles Police Department. I found all those things.

But I also found a vibrant and multilayered tapestry of communities and cultures. Here was an Ethiopian enclave replete with the smells and flavors of a proudly immigrant community. There was a street vendor selling hand-shaped pupusas made from her Salvadoran grandmother's recipe. Los Angeles is a rich amalgam formed from Leimert Park and its booming Black-led arts district and Glendale's Armenian bakeries and auto repair shops as well as Little Tokyo's bustling alleys filled with restaurants and Olvera Street's Día de los Muertos celebrations, and so much more.

Hollywood's white writers, surrounded for generations by this stunning ecology of cultures and traditions, utterly failed to capture it in their scripts and screenplays. The TV shows and movies that influenced global audiences, time and again, instead propagated ugly and reductive narratives about Black and Brown people, making them foils for white characters. Now that Hollywood has been shamed into allowing diverse creators to push their way in and pull up a few seats to the table, the results are promising and inspiring.

Over the past two decades there has been a transformation of the fictional stories that shape racial narratives. That transformation has been courageously led by filmmakers and TV showrunners of color rising up to tell our stories in complex ways, refusing to succumb to lazy stereotypes, and catering to increasingly diverse audiences. The transformation has also been spurred by the relentless pressure tactics that advocates and activists have utilized in naming and shaming Hollywood's racist offenders via in-depth studies or wry social media commentary.

But, just as in the transformations of our newsrooms, change has not come fast enough in Hollywood. The decision makers remain white. The executive suites remain entrenched in strict racial hierarchies. And, although there is much money to be made from films and TV shows with racially diverse casts, parity with our populations is a work in progress. White actors, writers, and directors continue to dominate our screens and our narratives, expecting gratitude for opening the door a crack to admit people of color.

Nothing less than a continuous striving for racial justice will do, a rising up from below—at least not until the centuries of dehumanizing story lines that Hollywood and mass media have profited from are balanced out.

Sharing stories about our lives and about one another is inherently human. But it matters who is telling the stories. *Our* stories can confirm our humanity, while the stories told *about us* can dehumanize us. Stories that have been shared and internalized about those of us with darker hues of skin have sought to turn us into monsters, fools, incompetents, and criminals. Those narratives have fueled centuries of oppression.

But *our* stories can change the equations of power.

When we write our own truths and amplify our complex realities in the face of an intransigent establishment, we tell *our* story.

When we own our narratives for public consumption, changing the plot points, expanding the complexities of our characters on big and small screens, we tell *our* story.

When we clap back at power using all the tools at our disposal, large and small, with patience, persistence, and vigilance, insisting on being heard and respected, we tell *our* story.

There are many vehicles for narrative change that I did not tackle in this book, such as storytelling, fiction, poetry, children's books, theater, visual art, music, stand-up comedy, music—and even architecture and the renaming of institutions and monuments that honor white supremacist leaders or dishonor Indigenous nations and people of color. All these forms of expression offer opportunities to counter and dismantle the influence of white supremacy, promote racial justice, and catalyze social and political transformation through narrative-shifting.

At each step, with each story, no matter what the medium, we gain a larger audience for our histories and cultures, painstakingly shifting the tide, pushing the cultural fabric of society to stretch itself and envelop us, calling in the gatekeepers and lawmakers to reckon with us and restore what has been lost during generations of omission, disinformation, violence, and indignity.

We now have the tools to organize collectively, confront abuses of power decisively, and transform communities and institutions on local and national levels. Black and Brown academics, activists, organizers, and influencers are using their platforms, their digital bullhorns, their classrooms, their books, to insist that our humanity must form the foundation of our depictions.

If all of this sounds vast and ambitious, it's because justice demands such commitment. And America owes it to us to keep that commitment.

EPILOGUE

There is a certain lucidity that emerges when one occupies the status of a minority. I recall feeling it starkly for the first time when I moved from the United Arab Emirates—a country where most people look like me—to Texas, one of the whitest parts of the United States.

I feel it each time I leave the multiracial spaces of Los Angeles and arrive in Boston to visit my in-laws.

I experience it when I leave the historically Black neighborhood where I live and cross the freeway to the whiter, wealthier parts of my adopted hometown of Pasadena, California.

The sensory shift that occurs when one moves from majority status into minority is instructive. Because our racial differences—superficial as they are on a biological level—are so visible to us, we often seek comfort in the conspicuous markers of skin color around which we aggregate.

I have begun to understand how the white right's fear of becoming a minority, of losing privilege and power—especially in recent years—reinforces racist narratives and structural racism. I can relate to the anxiety and anger, for I often feel it in white-dominated spaces. But I cannot relate to a thirst to dominate.

When people of color seek to correct the narratives that have been built up about us, we are not seeking power *over* another racial group. We are not seeking to bring George Orwell's *Animal Farm* to life by toppling racial hierarchies only to reproduce them in reverse order. We are seeking a reversal of injustice. We want space commensurate with our populations. We want racial equity. We want a collective liberation from oppression.

Eventually humanity may resemble my sons, two café-latte-colored mixed-race children. Already it's getting harder to discern racial difference in this nation. The 2020 US Census revealed a massive 276 percent jump in the "Two or More Races" population.[339]

There's no stopping the transformation of the nation. We are rising up. Black, Brown, Asian, Latino/a, and Indigenous people are reaching a critical mass, expanding our demographic presence in the United States, and representing what the racists fear when they dehumanize us. But this transformation need not generate fear or signify loss. Instead, it can be seen as a glorious evolution of not just who we are as individuals, but who we are—and can be—together.

ACKNOWLEDGMENTS

I AM A THREAD CONNECTING MY PARENTS TO MY CHIL-dren. It is because of the former—Ellen and Sham—that I have the education and privilege to put pen to paper. It is for the latter—Neal and Naveen—that I write and fight to envision a better world.

Alongside me has been my mentor, my best friend, my sounding board, my cheerleader, and my soulmate, Jim, whose partnership has guided me from past to present, and onward into the future.

I have needed to write this book for several years now. I felt it inside me. But it wasn't until City Lights editor Greg Ruggiero approached me that I was able to articulate just how badly my thoughts needed to spill out on paper. I thank Greg deeply for his guidance, thoughtful notes, and steady editing hand, and for helping me usher this book from mind into matter.

I am grateful to Rinku Sen, a racial justice leader whom I have looked up to for many years, for being so kind as to write the foreword to this book. And I am thankful for the many fellow journalists, academics, activists, organizers, and rabble-rousers whose words have formed the threads of this book, whose wisdom I have benefited from, and whose leadership I have been inspired by. It takes a large community to shift the tide toward a better tomorrow.

RESOURCES

THERE ARE NUMEROUS LEADING PROGRESSIVE ORGANIZATIONS, media outlets, and campaigns engaged in racial justice narrative-shifting work. This list is by no means comprehensive, but I hope it may serve as a starting point for those wanting to explore further.

Color of Change leads campaigns that build real power for Black communities, including media justice campaigns centered on ensuring accurate and diverse representations of Black people in media, ending inaccurate and racially biased news reporting, and achieving meaningful diversity and inclusion in Hollywood. More information at www. colorofchange.org.

Center for Cultural Power is a women-of-color, artist-led organization inspiring cultural workers to imagine a world where power is distributed equitably and where we live in harmony with nature. More information at www.culturalpower.org.

Fairness and Accuracy in Reporting (FAIR) is a national media watch group offering well-documented criticism of media bias and censorship. FAIR works with activists and journalists, providing constructive critiques and encouraging the public to contact media with their concerns, to become "media activists" rather than passive consumers of news. More information at www.FAIR.org.

Freedom Dreams, an interview podcast from the Detroit Justice Center, focuses on historical examples of experiments in liberation, and explores the work already being done to build an abolitionist world beyond police and incarceration. More information at www.freedomdreams podcast.com.

Liberation Ventures supports the reparations ecosystem through four levers: funding, technical assistance, connective tissue, and narrative change. More information at www.liberationventures.org.

Love Now Media is an empathy-centered multi-platform storytelling enterprise whose aim is to amplify acts of love at the intersection of social justice, wellness, and equity through video, audio, print, digital, and live events. More information at www.lovenowmedia.com.

MediaJustice is building a powerful grassroots movement for more just and participatory media, fighting for racial, economic, and gender justice in a digital age; and working toward a future where we are all connected, represented, and free. More information at www.mediajustice.org.

Narrative Initiative was established to equip leaders with the knowledge and skills necessary to harness the power of narrative for social change. Its aim is to weave the power of narrative with other social justice strategies to achieve long-term equity. More information at www.narrativeinitiative.org.

Othering and Belonging Institute at University of California, Berkeley advances groundbreaking approaches to transforming structural marginalization and inequality. The institute consists of scholars, organizers, communicators, researchers, artists, and policy makers committed to building a world where all people belong. More information at belonging.berkeley.edu.

Press On is a Southern media collective that catalyzes change and advances justice through the practice of movement journalism, with the aim of helping journalists and storytellers produce reporting driven by communities that are building power to create transformative social change. More information at www.presson.media.

Prism is an independent and nonprofit news outlet led by journalists of color, truth-tellers, organizers, and justice seekers committed to delivering in-depth and thought-provoking news and analysis. More information at www.prismreports.org.

Race Forward is an organization whose goal is to help movement building for racial justice, partnering with communities, organizations, and institutions to to advance racial justice. It is also the publisher of the news site Colorlines and presenter of Facing Race, the country's largest multiracial conference on racial justice. More information at RaceForward.org.

Radical Communicators Network (RadComms) is a community of practice for activists, organizers, and other change-makers working to build narrative power for social justice. More information at www.rad commsnetwork.org.

ReFrame builds narrative power by using potent technology to understand narratives across society in real time, gain strategic insight, and forecast arising opportunities to advance just narratives. More information at www.thisisreframe.org.

YES! Magazine is an independent, nonpartisan solutions journalism outlet. Through rigorous reporting on the positive ways communities are responding to social problems and insightful commentary that sparks constructive discourse, *YES!* inspires people to build a more just, sustainable, and compassionate world. More information at www.yesmagazine.org.

ENDNOTES

INTRODUCTION

1. William H. Frey, "The US will become 'minority white' in 2045, Census projects," Brookings Institution, March 14, 2018.
2. Shanelle Matthews, "The Role of Communications in Social Change," *Nonprofit Quarterly*, July 29, 2021.
3. Mark Turner, *The Literary Mind*, (UK: Oxford University Press, 1996), 4–5.
4. Jen Soriano, Joseph Phelan, Kimberly Freeman Brown, Hermelinda Cortés, Jung Hee Choi, "Creating an Ecosystem for Narrative Power," Medium.com, July 16, 2019.
5. Ibid.
6. National Center for Statistics and Analysis, "Traffic Safety Facts, 2006 Data," www.Nhtsa.gov, August 2009.
7. See RaceForward.org, "What is Racial Equity?" Accessed September 11, 2022.
8. Kimberly Yam, "'Fresh Off the Boat' Highlights Why the 'Bad Asian Driver' Stereotype Is Ridiculous," HuffPost.com, November 5, 2018.
9. Loretta Ross, "I'm a Black Feminist. I Think Call-Out Culture Is Toxic," *New York Times*, August 17, 2019.

10. bell hooks, *Black Looks: Race and Representation* (Boston: South End Press, 1992), 2.

11. john a. powell, "Racing into the Future," HuffPost.com, December 31, 2015.

ONE

12. "Bernhard Goetz shoots four youths on the subway," History.com, February 9, 2010.

13. Lawrie Mifflin, "Bob Grant Is Off Air Following Remarks On Brown's Death," *New York Times*, April 18, 1996.

14. Art Buchwald, "Free Speech, If It Pays," *New York Times*, April 23, 1996.

15. Sonali Kolhatkar, "New Film Examines Cult-Like Effects of Rightwing Media," *Rising Up With Sonali*, March 16, 2016.

16. Ibid.

17. Sarah McCammon, "Conservatives Weigh In on the Death of Rush Limbaugh," NPR.org, February 18, 2021.

18. Sonali Kolhatkar, "How Rush Limbaugh Laid the Groundwork for Trump," *Rising Up With Sonali*, February 18, 2021.

19. Ibid.

20. Kayleigh McEnany, Twitter post, Feb 17, 2021, 9:19 a.m.

21. Kayleigh McEnany, Twitter post, Feb 17, 2021, 3:23 p.m.

22. Kayleigh McEnany, Twitter post, August 29, 2012, 7:05 p.m.

23. Dayanita Ramesh, "Fox News Is Racist. Period." FreePress.net, November 25, 2019.

24. Ashley Parkey, Josh Dawsey, "Trump's cable cabinet: New texts reveal the influence of Fox hosts on previous White House," *Washington Post*, January 9, 2022.

25. Justin Horowitz, "Tucker Carlson not only promoted the white nationalist 'great replacement' theory, but repeatedly called on his audience to take action," Media Matters for America, May 16, 2022.

26. David Neiwert, "Explaining 'You Will Not Replace Us,' 'Blood and Soil,' 'Russia Is Our Friend,' and other catchphrases from torch-bearing marchers in Charlottesville," Southern Poverty Law Center, October 10, 2017.

27. Nicholas Confessore, Karen Yourish, "A Fringe Conspiracy Theory, Fostered Online, Is Refashioned by the G.O.P.," *New York Times*, May 15, 2022.

28. Tom Stafford, "How liars create the 'illusion of truth,'" BBC.com, October 26, 2016.

29. Pamela Brown, "Interview with Frank Meeink on his book Autobiography of a Recovering Skinhead," CNN.com, March 6, 2021.

30. Diana Falzone, "Fox News Insiders Rage Against Hiring 'Mini Goebbels' Kayleigh McEnany," The Daily Beast, March 2, 2021.

31. Sean McElwee and Jason McDaniel, "Do Racists Like Fox News, or Does Fox Make People Racist?" Fairness and Accuracy in Reporting, December 22, 2015.

32. Diego Graglia, "A 'Day of Happiness': Immigration Activists, Hispanic Press Relish Dobbs' Exit From CNN," *Feet in 2 Worlds*, November 13, 2009.

33. Travis L. Dixon, "A Dangerous Distortion of Our Families," Color of Change, December, 2017.

34. Paul Vitello, "Bob Grant, a Combative Personality on New York Talk Radio, Dies at 84," *New York Times*, January 2, 2014.

35. Ibid.

36. Peter Hart, "How Racist Do You Have to Be Before the *New York Times* Calls You a Racist?" FAIR.org, January 3, 2014.

37. Vitello, "Bob Grant."

38. Washington Post staff, "Full text: Donald Trump announces a presidential bid," *Washington Post*, June 16, 2015.

39. Michelle Ye Hee Lee, "Donald Trump's false comments connecting Mexican immigrants and crime," *Washington Post*, July 8, 2015.

40. Bianca Quilantan and David Cohen, "Trump tells Dem congress-women: Go back where you came from," Politico.com, July 14, 2019.

41. American Presidency Project, Tweets of July 14, 2019.

42. Keith Woods, "Report on Racism, but Ditch the Labels," NPR.org, July 17, 2019.

43. Ibid.

44. See NPR.org, "People, Keith Woods." Accessed September 11, 2022.

45. Paul Farhi. "'Racist' tweets? News media grapple with how to label Trump's latest attacks," *Washington Post*, July 15, 2019.

46. Sonali Kolhatkar, "How Election 2020 Exposed the Crisis in Journalism," *Rising Up With Sonali*, November 13, 2020.

47. David Bloom, "Love It or Hate It, the Trump Show Has Been Very Good for Media Business," Forbes.com, November 5, 2018.

48. Buchwald, "Free Speech If It Pays."

49. Paul Bond, "Leslie Moonves on Donald Trump: 'It May Not Be Good for America, but It's Damn Good for CBS,'" *Hollywood Reporter*, February 29 2016.

50. Ibid.

51. Katie Warren, "Les Moonves left CBS in September with a net worth of $700 million. Now, he won't get a dime of his $120 million severance," *Business Insider*, December 17, 2018.

52. Ibid.

53. Tom McCarthy, "Les Moonves resigns from CBS after six more women accuse him of sexual harassment," *The Guardian*, September 9, 2018.

54. Summer Harlow, Danielle K Kilgo, Ramón Salaverría, Víctor García-Perdomo, "Is the Whole World Watching? Building a Typology of Protest Coverage on Social Media from Around the World," *Journalism Studies*, June 12, 2020; Summer Harlow, "There's a double standard in how news media cover liberal and conservative protests," *Washington Post*, January 13, 2021.

55. Ibid.

56. Ibid.

57. Ibid.

58. Larry Buchanan, Quoctrung Bui, Jugal K. Patel, "Black Lives Matter May Be the Largest Movement in U.S. History," *New York Times*, July 3, 2020.

59. Stephanie Sugars, "At least 60 journalists have sued police following arrests, assaults at protests," US Press Freedom Tracker, December 16, 2021.

60. Jacey Fortin, "Minnesota Troopers Deleted Texts and Emails After Floyd Protests, Major Testifies," *New York Times*, September 6, 2021.

61. John Eligon, "Michael Brown Spent Last Weeks Grappling with Problems and Promise," *New York Times*, August 24, 2014.

62. New York Times Visual Investigations, "Police Misconduct & Racial Injustice in 2020," *New York Times*, March 11, 2021.

63. Adeshina Emmanuel, "Spurred by Black Lives Matter, Coverage of Police Violence Is Changing," *Nieman Reports*, January 28, 2021.

64. Ibid.

65. William H. Frey, "The nation is diversifying even faster than predicted, according to new census data," Brookings Institution, July 1, 2020.

66. Gabriel Arana, "Decades of Failure," *Columbia Journalism Review*, Fall 2018.

67. "The Status of Women of Color in the U.S. News Media 2018," Women's Media Center, March 6, 2018.

68. Ibid.

69. Gabe Schneider, "U.S. newsrooms are very white. So are the critics and the journalists that cover them," Poynter Institute for Media Studies, December 4, 2020.

70. Susan Goldberg, "For Decades, Our Coverage Was Racist. To Rise Above Our Past, We Must Acknowledge It," *National Geographic*, March 12, 2018.

71. Mike Fannin, "The truth in Black and white: An apology from The Kansas City Star," *Kansas City Star*, December 22, 2020.

72. Los Angeles Times Editorial Board. "An examination of The Times' failures on race, our apology and a path forward," *Los Angeles Times*, September 27, 2020.

73. Ibid.

TWO

74. Sonali Kolhatkar, "Featuring Black Lives Matter Activists Patrisse Cullors and Jasmine Richards," *Uprising with Sonali*, December 22, 2014.

75. Ibid.

76. Ibid.

77. Leah Asmelash, "How Black Lives Matter went from a hashtag to a global rallying cry," CNN.com, July 26, 2020.

78. Kolhatkar, "Featuring Black Lives Matter Activists Patrisse Cullors and Jasmine Richards."

79. Malkia Devich-Cyril in conversation with Susan Smith Richardson, "What role does media play in writing on race?" Center for Public Integrity, August 27, 2020.

80. Sonali Kolhatkar, "Featuring Black Lives Matter Co-founder Patrisse Cullors," *Uprising with Sonali*, July 1, 2015.

81. Ibid.

82. Ibid.

83. Gabriel Thompson, "How the Right Made Racism Sound Fair— and Changed Immigration Politics," Colorlines.com, September 13, 2011.

84. Monica Novoa, "Drop the I-Word Campaign Calls on the Associated Press to Remove the Term 'Illegal Immigrant' from Its Stylebook," Race Forward: The Center for Racial Justice Innovation, November 14, 2011.

85. Paul Colford, "'Illegal immigrant' No More," Associated Press, April 2, 2013.

86. Interview with author, June 27, 2022.

87. "Governor Newsom Signs Suite of Legislation to Support California's Immigrant Communities and Remove Outdated Term 'Alien' from State Codes," Office of Governor Gavin Newsom, September 24, 2021.

88. Bill Keller, "Inmate. Parolee. Felon. Discuss." The Marshall Project, April 1, 2015.

89. Scott Simon, "ESPN's Howard Bryant On 'Full Dissidence,'" Npr.org, *Weekend Edition*, Saturday, January 18, 2020.

90. Ibid.

91. Ibid.

92. Sonali Kolhatkar, "Full Dissidence: Notes from an Uneven Playing Field," *Rising Up With Sonali*, February 7, 2020.

93. Ibid.

94. Ibid.

95. Ibid.

96. Ibid.

97. Ibid.

98. Sonali Kolhatkar, "A New Podcast Aims to Shift the Narrative on Police Abolition by Centering Movement Voices," *YES! Magazine*, November 16, 2021.

99. Ibid.

100. See Anchor.fm, "How Can You Shut Down Your City Jail?" Accessed September 11, 2022.

101. J. David Goodman, "A Year After 'Defund,' Police Departments Get Their Money Back," *New York Times*, October 10, 2021.

THREE

102. hooks, *Black Looks*, 2.

103. "Cops Don't Stop Violence: Combating Narratives Used to Defend Police Instead of Defunding Them," Community Resource Hub and Interrupting Criminalization, July 26, 2021.

104. "Police More Likely to Use Force on Blacks than Whites, Study Shows," Center for Policing Equity, July 12, 2016.

105. Timothy Bella, "Police slow to engage with gunman because 'they could've been shot,' official says," *Washington Post*, May 27, 2022.

106. Madison Czopek, "Armed campus police do not prevent school shootings, research shows," Poynter Institute for Media Studies, June 1, 2022.

107. Radley Balko, "Study shows deep racial division when it comes to attitudes about cops—but it's driven by experience," *Washington Post*, December 20, 2016.

108. Chimamanda Ngozi Adichie, "The Danger of a Single Story," Ted.com, July 2009.

109. Alyssa Rosenberg, "How Police Censorship Shaped Hollywood," *Washington Post*, October 23, 2016.

110. Adrian Horton, "'The uprisings opened up the door': the TV cop shows confronting a harmful legacy," *The Guardian,* April 24, 2021.

111. James Hibberd, "Damon Lindelof gives his first deep-dive interview for HBO's Watchmen," Entertainment Weekly, September 18, 2019.

112. "Damon Lindelof on 'Watchmen' Police Narratives & Defund the Police Conversations," Close Up with The Hollywood Reporter, September 11, 2020.

113. Ibid.

114. Alan Neuhauser, "A Black Cop on the Silver Screen," *U.S. News and World Report*, July 26, 2016.

115. "Our Favorite Black TV Cops," *Essence*, October 29, 2020.

116. Seve Chambers, "The Rise of Black Cops and Policing Films," Black Art in America, November 23, 2019.

117. "Normalizing Injustice: The Dangerous Misrepresentations that Define Television's Scripted Crime Genre," Color of Change, January 2020.

118. Ibid.

119. Maya Williams, "Casting Black People as Cops Will Not Stop Black People from Dying," BlackGirlNerds.com, June 24, 2020.

120. Ibid.

121. Dave Nemetz, "L.A.'s Finest Review: Call In the Bomb Squad for This Loud, Dumb Cop Drama," TVLine.com.

122. "Normalizing Injustice," April 29, 2019.

123. Constance Grady, "How 70 years of cop shows taught us to valorize the police," Vox.com, April 12, 2021.

124. Ibid.

125. Ibid.

126. Tatiana Siegel, "Hollywood and the Police: A Deep, Complicated and Now Strained Relationship," *Hollywood Reporter*, July 1, 2020.

127. Steven Zeitchik, "CBS is remaking its police shows for the Black Lives Matter era," *Washington Post*, October 14, 2020.

128. Ibid.

129. Darnell Hunt, "Race in the Writers Room: How Hollywood Whitewashes the Stories that Shape America," Color of Change, October 2017.

130. Sonali Kolhatkar, "How Pervasive Is White Domination of TV Writers' Rooms?" *Rising Up With Sonali*, November 8, 2017.

131. Ibid.

132. Ibid.

133. Hunt, "Race in the Writers Room."

134. Steve Rose, "'I promised Brando I would not touch his Oscar': the secret life of Sacheen Littlefeather," *The Guardian*, June 3, 2021.

135. Ibid.

136. Aaron Morrison, "No 'John Wayne Day' in California Because He Was a White Supremacist," Mic.com, April 29, 2016.

137. Eli Rosenberg, "'I believe in white supremacy': John Wayne's notorious 1971 Playboy interview goes viral on Twitter," *Washington Post*, February 20, 2019.

138. Nadra Kareem Nittle, "5 Common Indigenous Stereotypes in Film and Television," ThoughtCo, January 6, 2021.

139. Nadra Kareem Nittle, "5 Common Black Stereotypes in TV and Film," ThoughtCo, March 6, 2021.

140. Gwen Aviles, "Latinos 'face an epidemic of invisibility' in film. A new report unpacks how Hollywood falls short in diversity," Insider.com, September 16, 2021.

141. Darnell Hunt and Ana-Christina Ramón, "Hollywood Diversity Report 2021, Pandemic in Progress. Part 1: Film," University of California, Los Angeles, 2021; Darnell Hunt and Ana-Christina Ramón, "Hollywood Diversity Report 2021, Pandemic in Progress. Part 2: Television," University of California, Los Angeles, 2021.

142. Darnell Hunt and Ana-Christina Ramón, "Hollywood Diversity Report, Part 1: Film," UCLA College Division of Social Sciences, February 6, 2020; Darnell Hunt and Ana-Christina Ramón, "Hollywood Diversity Report, Part 2: Television," UCLA College Division of Social Sciences, October 22, 2020.

143. Sonali Kolhatkar, "Comedian Hari Kondabolu Uses Humor to Talk About Race and Politics," *Rising Up With Sonali*, March 30, 2018.

144. Ibid.

145. Rebecca Sun, "Academy Apologizes to Sacheen Littlefeather for Her Mistreatment at the 1973 Oscars," *Hollywood Reporter*, August 15, 2022.

146. Ibid.

147. Caitlin O'Kane, "Sacheen Littlefather's sisters say she was not Native American. The actress had disputed similar claims before," CBS, October 24, 2022.

FOUR

148. Brian Moylan, "Black-ish takes on police brutality in a 'very special episode,'" *The Guardian*, February 24, 2022.

149. Rasha Ali, "'We just want to be seen': 'Black-ish' creator Kenya Barris, Anthony Anderson reflect on show's legacy," *USA Today*, April 10, 2022.

150. Julia Stoll, "Black-ish TV viewers in the U.S. 2018, by ethnicity," Statista.com, January 13, 2021.

151. Mikey O'Connell, "'Fresh Off the Boat' Creator on Breaking Diversity Rules on Broadcast TV: 'Everything Has Changed,'" *Hollywood Reporter*, April 5, 2019; Lynette Rice, "'Reservation Dogs': How Sterlin Harjo, Taika Waititi and the Cast Created a Fresh Take on Native American Life," Deadline.com, June 9, 2022.

152. Angie Han, "'Mo' Review: Mo Amer and Ramy Youssef's Netflix Comedy Is an Incisive Portrait of Palestinian-American Life," *Hollywood Reporter*, August 23, 2022; Max Bennett, "'Abbott Elementary' Wins 2 Primetime Emmys, Bringing Gold to Philly," Patch.com, September 13, 2022.

153. Ewan MacAskill, "Oscar Grant shooting: officer found guilty of involuntary manslaughter," *The Guardian*, July 8 2010; Rory Carroll, "Fruitvale Station's success a 'surprise' for first-time director Ryan Coogler," *The Guardian*, July 30, 2013.

154. Tom Seymour, "Fruitvale Station's Michael B Jordan: 'African-Americans aren't allowed to be real people,'" *The Guardian*, June 7, 2014.

155. Sonali Kolhatkar, "Fruitvale Station Humanizes Young Black Men Through Intimate Portrayal of Oscar Grant's Last Day," *Uprising Radio*, July 18, 2013.

156. Ibid.

157. Ibid.

158. Ibid.

159. Sonali Kolhatkar, "AFFRM Offers New Model for Black Indie Filmmakers," *Uprising Radio*, March 9, 2011.

160. Ibid.

161. Ibid.

162. Ibid.

163. Saba Hamedy, "A look at 'Selma' at the box office," *Los Angeles Times*, March 5, 2015.

164. Ava DuVernay, Twitter post, Dec 30, 2019, 1:07 p.m., et seq.

165. Veronica Wells, "On ARRAY's 10th Anniversary, Ava DuVernay Reflects on a Decade of Disruption & Her Own Unconscious Bias," *Essence*, December 10, 2021.

166. John Hudson, "In Middle Earth, Must All Hobbits Be White?" *The Atlantic*, November 30, 2010.

167. Christobel Hastings, "House of the Dragon v The Rings of Power: the major difference between the two prequels is the diversity," *Stylist*, September 14, 2022.

168. Lester Fabian Brathwaite, "House of the Dragon star Steve Toussaint thinks if dragons can fly, then Lord Velaryon can be Black," *Entertainment Weekly*, August 22, 2022.

169. Erik Gruenwedel, "Shonda Rhimes Highlights Diversity Ahead of 'Bridgerton: Season 2' Debut," Media Play News, March 22, 2022.

170. Bethonie Butler, "'Bridgerton's Golda Rosheuvel peels back Queen Charlotte's layers," *Washington Post*, March 30, 2022; Ankita Rao, "Bridgerton's South Asian representation is wonderfully anachronistic," *The Guardian*, April 6, 2022.

171. Mckenzie Jean-Philippe, "Bridgerton Doesn't Need to Elaborate on Its Inclusion of Black Characters," OprahDaily.com, December 29, 2020.

172. Regina Gunapranata, "The Case for Joy in BIPOC Stories," *YES! Magazine*, June 6, 2022.

173. Ibid.

174. E. J. Dickson, "Racists Are Worried About the Historical Accuracy of Mermaids," RollingStone.com, September 14, 2022.

175. Jody Serrano, "Twitter Bans Weirdo Who Shared Racist Video Changing Halle Bailey's Ariel from Black to White," Gizmodo, September 14, 2022.

176. Remy Tumin, "A New Ariel Inspires Joy for Young Black Girls: 'She Looks Like Me,'" *Washington Post*, September 14, 2022.

177. Dawn Chmielewski, "Lin-Manuel Miranda's 'Hamilton' Crashes Broadway's Billion-Dollar Club," Forbes.com, June 8, 2020.

178. Steven Zeitchik, "Why Disney Plus's July 4 streaming of 'Hamilton' is historic," *Washington Post*, June 24, 2020.

179. Ishmael Reed, "'Hamilton: the Musical': Black Actors Dress Up like Slave Traders…and It's Not Halloween," *CounterPunch*, August 21, 2015.

180. Hua Hsu, "In 'The Haunting of Lin-Manuel Miranda,' Ishmael Reed Revives an Old Debate," *The New Yorker*, January 9, 2019.

181. Sonali Kolhatkar, "Does Hamilton Musical Whitewash Enslavers?" *Rising Up With Sonali*, July 10, 2020.

182. Drew Grant, "Founding Father: 'Hamilton' Star Daveed Diggs on Being in the Room Where It Happens," *The Observer*, March 15, 2016.

183. Ashley Lee, "With 'In the Heights,' Jon M. Chu disrupts the movie musical. Here's how he did it," *Los Angeles Times*, June 3, 2021.

184. Jasmine Haywood, "In the Heights exemplified the ugly colorism I've experienced in Latinx communities," Vox.com, June 18, 2021.

185. Roland S. Martin, "Roland roasts Maher, Paul Begala for their 'arrogant' dismissing of Afro Latinos 'Heights' erasure," Roland Martin Unfiltered Daily Digital Show, June 21, 2021.

186. Rosa Clemente, Twitter post, Dec 2, 2021, 9:15 a.m.

187. Ibid.

188. Rosa Cartagena. "Who Does 'West Side Story' Really Serve?" Bitch Media, March 25, 2022.

189. Mary Dettloff, "UMass Amherst Doctoral Student Recounts Experience as Associate Producer on 'Judas and the Black Messiah,'" UMass.edu, March 17, 2021.

190. "Judas and the Black Messiah," RottenTomatoes.com. Accessed September 19, 2020.

191. Mark Kermode, "Judas and the Black Messiah review—truly gripping Black Panther drama," *The Guardian*, March 14, 2021.

192. Sonali Kolhatkar, "New Film About Fred Hampton Showcases FBI Malfeasance," *Rising Up With Sonali*, February 23, 2021.

193. Cindy Y. Rodriguez, "Day of the Dead trademark request draws backlash for Disney," CNN.com, May 11, 2013.

194. Sonali Kolhatkar, "Chicano Artists Resist Commercialization of Día de los Muertos," *YES! Magazine*, October 28, 2021.

195. Gustavo Arellano, "Lalo Alcaraz Creates Amazing 'Muerto Mouse' Cartoon in Response to Disney 'Día De Los Muertos' Fiasco," *OC Weekly*, May 8, 2013.

196. Kolhatkar, "Chicano Artists."

197. Ben Child, "Disney drops bid to trademark Day of the Dead," *The Guardian*, May 8, 2013.

198. Jordan Riefe, "How 'Coco' Turned from Controversial to Respectful of Mexican Culture," *Hollywood Reporter*, November 3, 2017.

199. Kolhatkar, "Chicano Artists."

200. Luis Gomez, "Oscars 2018: How SDSU alumnus Lalo Alcaraz helped 'Coco' feel Mexican," *San Diego Union-Tribune*, March 5, 2018.

201. Devan Coggan, "Pixar's 'Coco' unveils all-Latino voice cast, character details," *Entertainment Weekly*, June 6, 2017.

202. Kolhatkar, "Chicano Artists."

203. Christi Carras, "Oscars promise change after Ava DuVernay, David Oyelowo say voters sabotaged 'Selma,'" *Los Angeles Times*, June 5, 2020.

204. Scott Feinberg, "Oscar Voter Reveals Brutally Honest Ballot: 'There's No Art to 'Selma,' 'Boyhood' [Is] 'Uneven,'" *Hollywood Reporter*, February 18, 2015.

205. Samantha Grossman, "Almost All the Oscars Nominees Are White," Time.com, January 15, 2015.

206. April Reign, Twitter post, Jan 15, 2015, 5:56 a.m.

207. Reggie Ugwu, "The Hashtag That Changed the Oscars: An Oral History," *New York Times*, February 6, 2020.

208. Seamus Kirst, "#OscarsSoWhite: a 10-point plan for change by the hashtag's creator," *The Guardian*, February 25, 2016.

209. Ibid.

210. Ugwu, "The Hashtag."

211. Ibid.

212. Sonali Kolhatkar, "How Pervasive Is White Domination of TV Writers' Rooms?" *Rising Up With Sonali*, November 8, 2017.

213. Sonali Kolhatkar, "Latest Diversity Report Shows Movie Writers Still Too White," *Rising Up With Sonali*, April 1, 2022.

214. Kolhatkar, "How Pervasive."

215. Rebecca Ford, "#ChangeHollywood: Michael B. Jordan, Color of Change Launch Roadmap to Inclusion," *Hollywood Reporter*, July 23, 2020.

216. Ibid.

FIVE

217. Brooke Auxier, "Social media continue to be important political outlets for Black Americans," Pew Research Center, December 11, 2020.

218. Ibid.

219. André Wheeler, "Ten years of Black Twitter: a merciless watchdog for problematic behavior," *The Guardian*, December 23, 2019.

220. Clay Risen, "George Holliday, Who Taped Police Beating of Rodney King, Dies at 61," *New York Times*, September 22, 2021.

221. Ibid.

222. Azi Paybarah, "How a teenager's video upended the police department's initial tale," *New York Times*, April 20, 2021.

223. Darnella Frazier, Facebook post, May 25, 2020.

224. Nicholas Bogel-Burroughs and Marie Fazio, "Darnella Frazier captured George Floyd's death on her cellphone. The teenager's video shaped the Chauvin trial," *New York Times*, July 7, 2021.

225. Joe Hernandez, "Read This Powerful Statement from Darnella Frazier, Who Filmed George Floyd's Murder," NPR.org, May 26, 2021.

226. Elahe Izadi, "Darnella Frazier, the teen who filmed George Floyd's murder, awarded a Pulitzer citation," *Washington Post*, June 11, 2021.

227. Deen Freelon, Lori Lopez, Meredith D. Clark, and Sarah J. Jackson, "How Black Twitter and other social media communities interact with mainstream news," Knight Foundation, 2018.

228. Emily Wax-Thibodeaux, "Ferguson timeline: What's happened since the Aug. 9 shooting of Michael Brown," *Washington Post*, November 21, 2014.

229. Donovan X. Ramsey, "The Truth About Black Twitter," *The Atlantic*, April 10, 2015.

230. Sarah Jackson and Brooke Foucault Welles, "#Ferguson Is Everywhere: Initiators in Emerging Counterpublic Networks," *Information, Communication, and Society*, December 29, 2016.

231. John O'Neill, "Who Guided the National Debate on Ferguson?" Northeastern University, College of Arts, Media, and Design, January 18, 2016.

232. Ibid.

233. Deen Freelon et al., "How Black Twitter."

234. Deen Freelon, Charlton D. McIlwain, and Meredith D. Clark, "Beyond the Hashtags: #Ferguson, #BlackLivesMatter and the online struggle for offline justice," Center for Media and Social Impact, February 29, 2016.

235. Ibid.

236. Ibid.

237. Kate Arthur, "#MeToo Founder Tarana Burke on Weinstein Verdict: 'Implications Reverberate Far Beyond Hollywood,'" *Variety*, February 24, 2020.

238. Jodi Kantor, Megan Twohey, "Harvey Weinstein Paid Off Sexual Harassment Accusers for Decades," *New York Times*, October 5, 2017.

239. Tarana Burke, "I Founded 'Me Too' in 2006. The Morning It Went Viral Was a Nightmare," *Time Magazine*, September 14, 2021.

240. Ibid.

241. Ibid.

242. Tarana Burke, Instagram post, October 15, 2017.

243. Erynn Chambers TikTok account @Rynnstar. Accessed August 1, 2022.

244. Shelby Heinrich, "A Woman On TikTok Sang A Song Calling Out People For Using Racist Statistics, And It's Gone Super Viral," Buzzfeed.com, June 20, 2022.

245. Amber D. Dodd, "Gut-wrenching book highlights digital oppression of Black women," *National Catholic Reporter*, July 24, 2021.

246. Sonali Kolhatkar, "Misogynoir Transformed: Black Women's Digital Resistance," *Rising Up With Sonali*, June 29, 2021.

247. Janet Mock, Twitter post, May 15, 2012, 5:07 a.m.

248. Sonali Kolhatkar, "Misogynoir."

249. Janet Mock, "Solidarity & Sisterhood: My Journey (So Far) with #GirlsLikeUs," JanetMock.com, May 28, 2012.

250. Al Baker and Nate Schweber, "Woman Dies in a Brooklyn Fire That Is Deemed Suspicious," *New York Times*, May 12, 2012.

251. Kendall Trammell, "'Pose' director and trans woman Janet Mock makes history with a multi-year Netflix deal," CNN.com, June 19, 2019.

252. Claire Valentine, "Janet Mock on Why FX's 'Pose' Is 'Deeply Revolutionary,'" *Paper Magazine*, July 3, 2018.

253. Sonali Kolhatkar, "Misogynoir."

254. Ibid.

255. Taylor Lorenz, "The Original Renegade," *New York Times*, February 13, 2020.

256. Rebecca Jennings, "A super-famous TikTok star appeared on Jimmy Fallon. It didn't go great," Vox.com, March 30, 2021.

257. Noah Darden, Twitter post, March 30, 2021, 2:45 p.m.

258. Sara Delgado, "After Addison Rae Backlash, Jimmy Fallon Hosted Black TikTok Dancers on 'The Tonight Show,'" Teen Vogue, April 6, 2021.

259. Jonah E. Bromwich, "Everyone Is Canceled," *New York Times*, June 28, 2018.

260. Abby Ohlheiser, "The 96 hours that brought down Milo Yiannopoulos," *Washington Post*, February 21, 2017.

261. Ella Nilsen, "Richard Spencer had speeches scheduled at 2 colleges, and they've both uninvited him," Vox.com, August 16, 2017.

262. Emily A. Vogels, Monica Anderson, Margaret Porteus, Chris Baronavski, Sara Atske, Colleen McClain, Brooke Auxier, Andrew Perrin, Meera Ramshankar, "Americans and 'Cancel Culture': Where Some See Calls for Accountability, Others See Censorship, Punishment," Pew Research Center, May 19, 2021.

263. Peggy Noonan, "The Culture War Is a Leftist Offensive," *Wall Street Journal*, July 8, 2021.

264. Kali Holloway, "The Great Hypocrisy of Right-Wingers Claiming 'Cancel Culture,'" *The Nation*, March 19, 2021.

265. Ta-Nehisi Coates, "The Cancellation of Colin Kaepernick," *New York Times*, November 22, 2019.

266. See www.markey.senate.gov/imo/media/doc/ajopta.pdf. Accessed September 20, 2022.

267. Elizabeth Dwoskin, Nitasha Tiku, Craig Timberg, "Facebook's race-blind practices around hate speech came at the expense of Black users, new documents show," *Washington Post*, November 21, 2021.

268. Ibid.

269. Patti Sweet, "Google and Twitter Don't Want Us to Talk About Racism," *Health Affairs*, February 11, 2022.

270. Brian Contreras, Marisa Martinez, "Fed up with TikTok, Black creators are moving on," *Los Angeles Times*, September 16, 2021.

271. Ibid.

272. Ibid.

273. Abby Ohlheiser, "Welcome to TikTok's endless cycle of censorship and mistakes," *MIT Technology Review*, July 13, 2021.

274. Kevin Roose, "Social Media Giants Support Racial Justice. Their Products Undermine It," *New York Times*, June 19, 2020.

SIX

275. Interview with author, June 27, 2022.

276. Jacey Fortin, "Critical Race Theory: A Brief History," *New York Times*, November 8, 2021.

277. Molly Minta, "Inside Mississippi's only class on critical race theory," *Mississippi Today*, February 2, 2022.

278. Keisha Rowe, "Lawmakers are pushing to ban critical race theory in all Mississippi classrooms," *Mississippi Clarion Ledger*, January 20, 2022.

279. Molly Minta, "Inside Mississippi."

280. Sonali Kolhatkar, "'All the Real Indians Died Off' and 20 Other Myths About Native Americans," *Rising Up With Sonali*, October 3, 2016.

281. Sonali Kolhatkar, "Children's Author Tells the True Story of Columbus' Exploits," *YES! Magazine*, October 10, 2021.

282. Ibid.

283. Ibid.

284. Ibid.

285. See www.orielmariasiu.com.

286. Meryl Kornfield, "California becomes first state to require ethnic studies for high school graduation," *Washington Post*, October 9, 2021.

287. Brooke Donald, "Stanford study suggests academic benefits to ethnic studies courses," *Stanford News*, January 12, 2016.

288. Matt Barnum, "As states place new limits on class discussions of race, research suggests they benefit students," Chalkbeat.org, July 8, 2021.

289. Kolhatkar, "Children's Author."

290. Ibid.

291. Fortin, "Critical Race Theory."

292. Payne Hiraldo, "The Role of Critical Race Theory in Higher Education," *The Vermont Connection*, January 2010.

293. Travis Gibson, Joe McLean, "DeSantis lashes out at 'critical race theory' in push to overhaul Florida's civics curriculum," News4Jax, March 18, 2021.

294. Diane Roberts, "DeSantis aims to scare academics. Unfortunately, it's working," *Washington Post*, August 18, 2022.

295. Florida House of Representatives, "CS/HB 7—Individual Freedom," MyFloridaHouse.gov, July 1, 2022.

296. Sonali Kolhatkar, "How Scholars Are Countering Well-Funded Attacks on Critical Race Theory," *YES! Magazine*, January 11, 2022.

297. Ibid.

298. Mike Gonzalez, "How the Grassroots Are Resisting CRT," The Heritage Foundation, July 27, 2021.

299. Alyce McFadden, "Secretive 'dark money' network launches anti–critical race theory campaign," OpenSecrets.org, June 30, 2021.

300. Brian Schwartz, "Business executives and wealthy Republican donors helped fund attacks on critical race theory during campaigns," CNBC.com, November 10, 2021.

301. Sonali Kolhatkar, "Is It Possible to Realize the Unfulfilled Promise of Juneteenth?" *Rising Up With Sonali*, June 16, 2022.

302. Ibid.

303. Ibid.

304. Sonali Kolhatkar, "Does It Matter That the Oscars Are Overwhelmingly White?" Truthdig.com, February 28, 2014.

305. Sara Sandrik, "Madera County Board of Education President resigns following backlash over social media post," ABC30.com, June 25, 2020.

306. Kim LaCapria, "Obama Took $2.6B from Veterans for Syrian Refugees," Snopes.com, April 25, 2016; Dan Evon, "Was 'Little Timmy Salutes the Flag' Banned by Facebook?" Snopes.com, October 30, 2015.

307. German Lopez, "Research says there are ways to reduce racial bias. Calling people racist isn't one of them," Vox.com, July 30, 2018.

308. Sonali Kolhatkar, "Beyond Cancel Culture: How to Hold Each Other Accountable—With Love," *YES! Magazine*, September 14, 2021.

309. Ngọc Loan Trân, "Calling IN: A Less Disposable Way of Holding Each Other Accountable," BGDBlog.org, December 18, 2013.

310. Kolhatkar, "Beyond Cancel Culture."

311. Ibid.

312. Christopher M. Tinson and Javiera Benavente, "Toward a Democratic Speech Environment," Association of American Colleges & Universities, 2017.

313. Kolhatkar, "Beyond Cancel Culture."

314. C. W. Dawson, "The writings of James Baldwin are important today," *Columbia Missourian*, December 10, 2019.

315. Sonali Kolhatkar, "Can We 'Agree to Disagree' in Order to Save Our Democracy?" *Rising Up With Sonali*, April 15, 2022.

316. Ibid.

317. David Broockman, Joshua Kalla, "Durably reducing transphobia: A field experiment on door-to-door canvassing," *Science*, April 8, 2016.

318. See NewConvo.org, "What Is Deep Canvassing?"

319. Wesley Lowery, "AOC's Fight for the Future," GQ.com, September 7, 2022.

320. NewConvo.org, "What Is Deep Canvassing?"

321. "How to Defeat Trump and Heal America: Deep Canvassing and Political Persuasion in the 2020 Presidential Election," PeoplesAction.org, September 2020.

322. Sonali Kolhatkar, "Is Biden's Presidency Achieving What Progressives Wanted?" *Rising Up With Sonali*, January 26, 2022.

323. Ibid.

CONCLUSION

324. Darnell Hunt, Ana-Christina Ramón, "Hollywood Diversity Report 2022, A New, Post-Pandemic Normal? Part 1: Film," University of California, Los Angeles, 2022.

325. Darnell Hunt, Ana-Christina Ramón, "Hollywood Diversity Report 2021, Pandemic in Progress. Part 1: Film," University of California, Los Angeles, 2021.

326. KK Ottesen, "Cornel West: Is America 'even capable of treating the masses of Black people with decency and dignity,'" *Washington Post*, August 11, 2020.

327. Frederick Douglass, "(1857) If There Is No Struggle, There Is No Progress," Blackpast.org, January 25, 2007.

328. Tracy Jan, Jena McGregor, Meghan Hoyer, "Corporate America's $50 billion promise," *Washington Post*, August 24, 2021.

329. Ibid.

330. White House Briefing Room, "Executive Order on Advancing Racial Equity and Support for Underserved Communities Through the Federal Government," WhiteHouse.gov, January 20, 2021.

331. Interview with author, June 27, 2022.

332. Sonali Kolhatkar, "New Film 'America's Family' Brings Immigration Injustices to Big Screen," *Rising Up With Sonali*, June 23, 2020.

333. Ibid.

334. Ibid.

335. Interview with author, June 27, 2022.

336. Ibid.

337. Elizabeth Grieco, "Newsroom employees are less diverse than U.S. workers overall," Pew Research Center, November 2, 2018.

338. See FreePress.net, "Diversity in Media Ownership."

EPILOGUE

339. Nicholas Jones, Rachel Mark, Roberto Ramirez, Merarys Ríos-Vargas, "2020 Census Illuminates Racial and Ethnic Composition of the Country," United States Census Bureau, August 12, 2021.

ABOUT THE AUTHOR

SONALI KOLHATKAR is the host and creator of *Rising Up With Sonali*, a weekly one-hour television and radio program covering news and politics, built on the foundation of her show *Uprising*, which became the longest-running drive-time radio show in Los Angeles hosted by a woman. *Rising Up With Sonali* airs on Pacifica stations KPFK in Los Angeles and KPFA in Berkeley, California, and on dozens of community radio stations, as well as Free Speech TV (Dish Network, DirecTV, Roku, Sling TV).

Kolhatkar is the racial justice editor at *YES! Magazine* and a writing fellow and senior correspondent for the Independent Media Institute's "Economy for All" project, where she writes a nationally syndicated weekly column about economic justice. Previously, she was a columnist for Truthdig.com.

With more than 20 years of journalistic experience, Kolhatkar has won awards at the Los Angeles Press Club including Best TV Anchor in 2015, Best Election Commentary in 2017, and Best National Commentary Political Online in 2022.

She has also been recognized by community organizations such as Hunger Action LA, South Asian Network, American-Arab Anti-Discrimination Committee, and Koreatown Immigrant Workers Alliance.

In 2015 she was named "Historian of the Lions" in an award from Center for the Study of Political Graphics. In 2004, she won the Phenomenal Woman Award from the California State University, Northridge women's studies department. In 2021, she joined the board of directors of Justice Action Center, a nonprofit organization furthering immigrant justice through litigation and storytelling.

Kolhatkar has also reported internationally from the World Social Forums in Porto Alegre, Brazil, and Mumbai, India; the war zones of Kabul, Herat, and Kandahar in Afghanistan; the historic UN COP 21 climate meeting in Paris; and her birthplace, Dubai, UAE. Her national reporting has taken her to numerous political conventions in election years, the Left Forum in New York, the People's Summit in Chicago, the great immigration marches of 2006, the Women's March of 2017, and more.

In 2000, she became a founding co-director of the Afghan Women's Mission a US-based nonprofit organization that supports the work of the Revolutionary Association of the Women of Afghanistan (RAWA). This led her to write the 2006 book *Bleeding Afghanistan: Washington, Warlords, and the Propaganda of Silence* (Seven Stories Press) with co-author James Ingalls. She has also contributed writings to the anthologies *Aftermath: Life in Post-Roe America*, *September 11, 2001: Feminist Perspectives*, and *Stop the Next War Now! Effective Responses to Violence & Terrorism*, and has spoken at hundreds of college campuses and community centers about media reform, social movements, activism, racial justice, women's rights, and foreign policy.

Kolhatkar has a master's degree in astronomy from the University of Hawaii and two undergraduate degrees in physics and astronomy from the University of Texas at Austin. After graduation she briefly worked at California Institute of Technology on NASA's Spitzer Science Telescope. She describes her transition from science to journalism in her 2014 Tedx talk, "My journey from astrophysicist to radio host."

Originally from India and born and raised in Dubai, Kolhatkar is a prolific visual artist and crafter, plays ukulele and bass, bakes cakes and confections, and lives with her husband, two sons, and her parents in Pasadena, California.

ALSO AVAILABLE IN THE OPEN MEDIA SERIES

Twenty Dollars and Change
Harriet Tubman and the Ongoing Fight for Racial Justice and Democracy
By Clarence Lusane, Foreword by Kali Holloway

Women Who Change the World
Stories from the Fight for Social Justice
By Lynn Marie Lewis, Featuring Malkia Devich-Cyril, Priscilla Gonzalez, Terese Howard, Hilary Moore, Vanessa Nosie, Roz Pelles, Loretta Ross, Yomara Velez, and Betty Yu

Build Bridges, Not Walls
A Journey to a World Without Borders
By Todd Miller

No Fascist USA!
The John Brown Anti-Klan Committee and Lessons for Today's Movements
By Hilary Moore and James Tracy, Foreword by Robin D. G. Kelley

Loaded
A Disarming History of the Second Amendment
By Roxanne Dunbar-Ortiz

Have Black Lives Ever Mattered?
By Mumia Abu-Jamal

United States of Distraction
Media Manipulation in Post-Truth America (And What We Can Do About It)
By Mickey Huff and Nolan Higdon, Foreword by Ralph Nader

Narrative of the Life of Frederick Douglass, an American Slave, Written by Himself
A New Critical Edition
By Angela Y. Davis

CITY LIGHTS BOOKS | OPEN MEDIA SERIES
Arm Yourself with Information